STEP BY STEP WE CLIMB TO FREEDOM

as given by the Ascended Masters

Volume 2
of the
Step By Step Series

Pearl Publishing
of Mount Shasta

Post Office Box 1290
Mount Shasta, California 96067

Books in this series:

STEP BY STEP WE CLIMB
STEP BY STEP WE CLIMB TO FREEDOM
STEP BY STEP WE CLIMB TO FREEDOM AND VICTORY

These books may be ordered from:

Pearl Publishing
of Mount Shasta
Post Office Box 1290
Mount Shasta, California 96067

See back page for additional information.

———————

Step By Step We Climb To Freedom (Volume 2)
Text, copyright © 1981, by M.S. Princess.
Cover Art, Pearl Publishing Logo, Step By Step Series Logo,
Introduction, and Subject Index copyright © 1990 by M.S. Princess.
All rights reserved.

Printed in the United States of America.

First printing: 1981   Third printing: 1985
Second Printing: 1983   Fourth printing: 1990

Cover art designed by Cindy and Dewey Reid.

Library of Congress Cataloging in Publication Data

Step by step we climb to freedom / as given by the Ascended Masters.
    p.   cm. — (The Step by step series ; v. 2)
    A Collection of discourses dictated by the various Ascended Masters.
    Bibliography: p.
    ISBN 0-9619770-2-7 (pbk.)   ISBN 0-9619770-4-3 (set)

    1. Spirit writings.   I. Series.
BF1290.S73   1990
133.9'3—dc19   88-18011
                                                        CIP

A NOTE OF GRATITUDE

I wish to express my deepest gratitude to all the sincere students of the Light whose earnest desire has made the release of this book possible, and to the great Ascended Ones, whose book this is, and whose assistance has been and is unlimited.

—*Pearl*

DEDICATION

This Book is dedicated in deepest Eternal Love and Gratitude to our Beloved Master Saint Germain, Jesus, the Great Divine Director, the Great White Brotherhood, the Brotherhood of the Royal Teton, the Brotherhood of Mount Shasta, and those other Ascended Masters whose Loving Help and Assistance has been Direct and Without Limit.

The Ascended Master Saint Germain.

INTRODUCTION

"There is only one reality
and that is the living Presence of God within you."
—Saint Germain

For centuries in all parts of the world, among all races, in all cultures, there has existed the legend of a mystical brotherhood. The legend describes a secret fellowship, sometimes called the Great White Brotherhood, comprised of individuals who, throughout many lifetimes, have succeeded in mastering all aspects of earthly experience and who have then gone on to serve and assist humanity from a higher dimension, in complete attunement with the One God.

Known for their wise and benevolent use of intelligence, their commitment to serve the good in all men, and the power of their love and compassion, these brothers and sisters have demonstrated the way of perfect development and have ultimately mastered it. Not surprisingly, while in their physical embodiments, these men and women became the beloved Way-showers in their cultures. In the western, Christian world, Jesus and later St. Theresa of Avila were Way-showers. Among eastern traditions, Buddha and Lao Tze were revered as the guardians of the spiritual destiny of the people. In Europe, Saint Germain worked tirelessly to awaken the inner God Presence within the individual.

The written works of these revered saints share a common message: the kingdom of heaven is to be found within the individual. They assert that the experience of the God Presence within is one that can be cultivated, and that it must be cultivated if man hopes to achieve any lasting peace and happiness in this life. When, through meditation, prayer, and other spiritual disciplines, we put our attention on this inner God Presence, we grow into the real purpose of life itself, the joyous experience of unity with God and our fellow men.

You have in your hand a key to the path of development traveled by the saints and the great masters of many traditions. The discourses in this book are given by the Ascended Masters. They are called Ascended Masters because, having mastered human experience, they have ascended this earthly realm and now operate and serve from a higher dimension in God's creation. Unlike those who are called master in various parts of the world, but who function in the physical body, the Ascended Master is no longer physical, but operates in an immortal body made of light. His or Her sole desire and purpose is to serve and assist in illumining and raising the humanity of earth to the level of Mastery.

At appropriate times in every age, the Brotherhood of Ascended Masters delivers some needed instructions to humanity, and one of its own comes forth to perform that service. Some of these events, such as the activity at Lourdes, have been well known and well documented. All have carried a great blessing to the people of Earth, especially to those who have been fortunate enough to experience firsthand the wisdom and love of these emissaries of the Brotherhood.

Another assistance to humanity by the Ascended Masters began in the year 1930. In the late summer of that year, an American named Guy W. Ballard, who later came to be known as Godfre Ray King, decided to spend a few months reviewing and rededicating his life. At this time, Godfre found himself drawn to visit Mount Shasta in northern California, a mountain known for its majestic beauty and for the sanctified atmosphere it radiates. It was his habit to rise early in the morning, and he would then spend the day hiking and exploring. On one of these days, he stopped to take his lunch at a small stream. As he reached his cup into the water, he felt something like an electric current pass through his body, and he suddenly became aware that he was not alone. When he turned around, the Ascended Master Saint Germain stood before him. During the next few months, Godfre was frequently in the blessed presence of the Master. Thus began a course of instruction in which the intimate workings of the great laws of life were revealed to him. This instruction came to be known as the teachings of the Ascended Masters.

The knowledge and practices imparted to Godfre by Saint Germain were a revelation of teachings long held in secret by the Ascended Masters. These were presented in a systematic manner, with each instruction given as a necessary step in the development of the Christ Consciousness and the process of ascension. Saint Germain explained that the student must first accept and then come to experience the God Presence within himself. This inner reality Saint Germain calls the "I AM" Presence. He then gave Godfre instructions how to experience it directly through a technique of meditation, which Godfre describes in his book *Unveiled Mysteries.*

Godfre was then instructed in the unseen laws governing the use of the "I AM" Presence to develop the Christ Consciousness within man. According to Saint Germain, it was by Divine Decree that the men and women of this age should now be shown how to experience the Divine in every phase of human existence and ultimately become free from the wheel of re-embodiment to become Ascended Masters. The time had finally come to remove the shroud of mystery which has always surrounded self-mastery.

Through the application of this knowledge Godfre quickly raised himself to a level of spiritual development seldom seen in the western world. Godfre describes his experience and much of the instruction he was given by Saint Germain in his books *Unveiled Mysteries, The Magic Presence,* and the *I AM Discourses*[*] under his pen name, Godfre Ray King. It was the reading of these experiences, as well as Godfre's humility, love, and divine radiation, that attracted students from all walks of life throughout the world. Of those who were drawn to him, two of his most sincere students were Pearl Diehl (later Pearl Dorris) and Bob LeFevre. Both Pearl and Bob shared a deep desire and a commitment to further the Masters' divine work with humanity. When Godfre's ascension came in 1939, Saint Germain appeared to Bob and Pearl and requested that they render a certain service for him. The depth of their sincerity and dedication over the years had distinguished them to carry on the Master's work. As requested, they assembled a small group of sincere students. It was to this group that Saint Germain and the other Ascended Masters gave the Ascended Master discourses contained in the first two volumes of the *Step by Step Series.*

These are instructions for the attainment of self-mastery. In these discourses the Masters continue to reveal the true understanding of the spiritual laws of life and how to apply them. They also illumine the most crucial steps we will all take on our path to the Christ Consciousness and our ultimate ascension. In addition, and perhaps most importantly, these teachings are charged with the radiation of these magnificent Beings of Light.

The books in the *Step by Step* series are not the result of "channeling," hypnosis, or any other trance-like procedure. When Saint Germain, or other Ascended Masters would appear, they were visible in their bodies of light to Bob's inner vision. In addition, as the

---

[*] *Unveiled Mysteries, The Magic Presence,* and the *I AM Discourses* can be ordered from the Saint Germain Press, 1120 Stonehedge Drive, Schaumburg, Illinois 60194.

Masters would speak, letters of light would simultaneously flash before Bob's eyes. This assured tremendous accuracy, not only in recording the information being given, but in capturing the wonderful radiation of love that emanates from these Great Ones.

Volumes I and II contain discourses given by Saint Germain and other Ascended Masters to Bob and Pearl during their years of collaborative service from 1940 to 1949. Volume III is a collection of inspired talks given by Pearl in the 1970's and early 1980's in the living room of her home in Mt. Shasta. These have been transcribed from taped recordings and offer a keen insight into the practical application of the Ascended Master teachings from one who has been practicing them for over fifty years. When once asked to describe the source of the wisdom and insight that poured forth from her during these talks, Pearl answered that it was the result of deep attunement to the "raised consciousness of the Christ Principle."

Under the Masters' guidance, people from all parts of the world have found their way to Pearl's door. Literally thousands have come to listen and ask questions. In Pearl's presence one feels the love and humility of the Christ Consciousness radiating from her being. Her life has been one of dedicated service, and her time and effort has always been given freely and as a gift of love. Such service to mankind, based upon individual effort, is the cornerstone of the Ascended Master teachings and has been the focus of Pearl's life.

It is now possible for all of us to become the example of transcendent love and compassionate service that is our true destiny and the destiny of all those who would walk in the footsteps of the Masters. In the words of Saint Germain:

> Yours is the responsibility of your world—yours alone.
> Accept the responsibility in joy and happiness, with your feelings calm and determined, going forward. And I assure you, never will you lack for any good thing, and you will find the way opening before you and Ascended Master Friends springing up to stand by your side."

It is our deepest hope that the teachings and Divine radiation of this book will help all those who have been guided to its message to fully realize this blessed invitation.

CONTENTS

I. New Age Transition, by Saint Germain............15

II. Illumined Obedience, by Saint Germain.............26

III. Qualify With Perfection, by The Master Jesus........34

IV. The Love of an Arisen Master, by Mighty Victory....40

V. Be Natural—Be Happy, by Urlando..................42

VI. Steadfastness to Ideals, by Saint Germain and
The Goddess of Peace..........................47

VII. Clearing The Way, by Saint Germain................56

VIII. Your Sacred Trust, by K-17.......................65

IX. The Great Spiritual Lesson, by Saint Germain........67

X. Harmony—The Great Law of Life,
by Saint Germain and God Meru.................75

XI. You Are The Christ, by The Master Jesus............85

XII. A New Cycle, by Saint Germain and Urlando........92

XIII. The Inner Realms, by Saint Germain and Cyclopea.....100

XIV. The Dawn of the Golden Century, by Saint Germain...112

XV. A Kumara Brings a Warning,
Godfre introduces Khubal Kumara..............121

XVI. Godfre's Ascension, by Godfre.....................127

XVII. All Mankind Are One, by Saint Germain...........130

XVIII. The Law of the Attention, by Saint Germain........136

XIX. Man Moves On a Higher Spiral, by Cyclopea........146

XX. The Cosmic Hour, by The Mighty Elohim Arcturus....149

XXI. The I AM Presence, by The Presence...............155

XXII. Be a Sun of Light, by Saint Germain................167

XXIII. New Year's Eve With The Masters, by Arcturus.....174

XXIV. The Answer Is Love, by Lord Maitreya.............177

XXV. The Simple Pathway to Heaven, by Lord Maitreya...183

A Fiat, by Lord Maitreya..........................191

Subject Index.....................................192

Editorial Note

These discourses were received by Bob LeFevre as a steady stream of Letters of Light flashed before his inner vision by the Masters. As Bob received each discourse, he would read the words aloud. Sunny Widell, the editor of this volume, listened carefully and recorded each discourse verbatim in shorthand as Bob spoke the words. The only indications Sunny received of proper punctuation were the natural pauses in Bob's speech. Punctuation was reconstructed and revised as necessary, hours or days later when Sunny transcribed her shorthand notes.

The transcribed discourses were held by Pearl and Sunny as a sacred trust in their original form for many years until the prompting was received to publish them in a form suitable for the inspiration and guidance of new and developing students. Each discourse was reviewed and all passages of a private, personal, or historical nature were deleted, leaving only the Master's instructions on Divine Law and its application. Occasionally a chapter on a particular subject or point of law was created by compiling relevant paragraphs and passages from different discourses. This editorial process naturally resulted in some compromise to the smooth flow of the original discourses.

Dear reader, if you encounter an occasional error in grammar or punctuation, or if you find a paragraph that does not appear to flow as smoothly as the preceeding material, the editor asks for your patience and understanding. She has done her very best to preserve for you this priceless instruction free from human interference.

I

NEW AGE TRANSITION

by Saint Germain

Beloved Guardians of the Light:

I greet you with the Infinite Joy and Love at My command and bless you and thank you for every effort you have put forth and are making in carrying forward this Great Light. Truly today is one We shall never forget, and the many accomplishments will make it as a day of great rejoicing in time to come.

Does it seem strange to you that here in San Francisco I am drawing together another section of My Great Family? It is not strange, but rather, just a natural expression and expansion of the Light, for you beloved ones who are gathering around My Precious Children have gathered around before many times, and your sincerity and loyalty in your calls have opened the way again for a great service to be rendered.

Long have We searched for a group of people upon whom We could depend. Long have We labored. Long have the Messengers striven to find those who could be trusted—to find those who understood the Power of Silence and would give obedience in maintaining that silence.

In coming to you this evening I bring you greetings from the Host of Arisen Masters, those who are assisting and are aware of this special activity, of which I have charge, the Great Angelic Host, the Legions of Light, and also those in charge of the four elements. In the activities of building this New Golden Age, much will be accomplished if you pour forth your love to the little beings of the elements, who are quite different from you in many respects and yet very eager to serve in love.

At this particular time I would suggest decrees and blessings for the Forces of the Elements, particularly the salamanders and undines, which are the beings of the fire and water. Those two elementals, uncontrolled, have been known to cause the greatest havoc to mankind at times of cataclysmic action. It is fortunate that you have the opportunity of giving love to these beings who, in large measure, may find it possible to assist you.

You know, in many of the civilizations which have existed before upon Earth, still greater heights were reached than those enjoyed now by the majority of people in embodiment. Do you know how We judge the advancement and progress of Earth? Do you think it is by inventions? Do you think it is by fine buildings? No! The great civilizations have been those in which the greatest number of people lived closest to their God Presence within and were the happiest in so doing.

It does not take brains to win happiness, but Love! He who will call forth Love, the very Living Essence of Life Itself, the fount of all good from the I AM Presence, is fortunate indeed.

In much that has been accomplished we have been greatly encouraged, and with the wonderful inventions which will come forth We have the opportunity to build in the New Golden Age a civilization which has been undreamed of. You know, this is an amazing thing, many of the previous civilizations just before their collapse became very destructive, very vicious, but never have We found a civilization so complicated as the one in which humanity finds itself now.

Life is so simple, so magnificent, and the understanding of that life so easily understood, and yet the human mind has gone to work constantly to make it difficult for itself. Why? Only because of fear and greed. Mankind fears to let go, but constantly builds and builds human creation in its vain effort to find what is called "security." There is no security anywhere but in the arms of the Presence. And the ascension, the goal of everyone, is the only permanent security there is. Now that that understanding has come forth and the living proof been given, there will be many who will awaken as if from a drugged sleep and almost frantically turn to this Light. I think We have the means of that awakening in many almost prepared, and although to some it may be a great shock, still the blessing it will bring is beyond comprehension.

Blessed ones, the fragrance in this room which has been created by your love sent to Me is the most glorious thing. I thank you and bless you sincerely.

How We in the Arisen state long for the day when We may stand forth before you and hold you tangibly within our own embrace. Because of the density of the physical octave, that is not the course of wisdom at the present time, but yet We may do it some day. Your love, your earnestness and your humility is the doorway through which We pass to you.

Just one word of caution to all of you. Give no heed to any appearance, and certainly give no heed to any gossip. Gossip, of course, is merely one type of appearance. You see, actually any appearance, whether it be an appearance of good or an appearance of evil, has no power within itself, and only responds to the power which you give it. Therefore, if you become aware of something which you do not like, refuse acceptance to it. Know the Power of your Presence. Maintain harmony in your feelings and refuse acceptance to appearances. Sometimes you have to take a very strong stand, but even in your strong stand, be happy and harmonious.

With the limitless release of Cosmic Joy which has taken place many of mankind will become lifted, and those who are able to maintain that Joy in conscious action will find much less difficulty in obtaining their final Victory.

Tonight I have been drawing various currents of energy and lines of force through this room and as I speak the words through this blessed boy, students throughout the land and many illumined ones throughout the Earth will tune in and become aware of what is taking place. The activiy of the two Secret Rays to this Earth, brought in by Cosmos, shall now be felt more and more by mankind. The entire United States today has had unusual atmospheric conditions. Many have observed it. Before long the atmospheric conditions, even over your large cities, will be so clear that the very clarity will assist in freeing man's consciousness of many human things.

I have a rare treat in store for you tonight. The Great Master Urlando will speak to you:

Master Urlando speaks:

Saint Germain has brought to you the mightiest, all inclusive Laws of Life through His Messengers, who are known throughout the Cosmic Realms of space. He has brought this Truth to mankind, but only a comparative few have awakened to the reality. The hour has struck and they shall awake, for the way is here prepared. Rapidly, this tangible Truth will be given forth, and no one with any resemblance to reason will ever, in the large, deny the ecstatic Truth which "I AM."

The dawn of the next Age is about to burst forth in the land of America, and the reality of Light will be quickly established. Today came another great release of Cosmic Light, a portion of the New Dispensation which has been called for. This time the whole Earth was flooded, which means that a blending, harmonizing Power of Light will go into action to bring about the oneness of many races, of many lands and their people.

It is very interesting to Me to observe tonight, after such a few years away from this planet, the doubts and fears that inhabit the human consciousness. I have not seen anything like it for a long time, and I rejoice in this group here, for I see very little of that.

I believe it wise to say something to you concering those whom you may contact from time to time who seem to have the activity of sight, or second sight, or the All-Seeing Eye of God. Well, from all that I have been able to observe, approximately 85% of the people who inform you they have the All-Seeing Eye of God, have in reality a very vivid imagination, for the activity of the All-Seeing Eye of God has absolutely nothing of the psychic or astral in it; and beware of individuals who do not look you in the eye but constantly look elsewhere and see things. They are seeing things all right! They are seeing their own human creation!

You will find in many of the things coming forth in the New Golden Age that speed will seem to increase in many things. You see, knowing there is no time or space, speed becomes one with the Great Silence. Think about that.

I wish to thank you for receiving Me so graciously. Don't forget, I move with the speed of Light and come on the Ray of your own attention to Me.

Saint Germain continues:

I rejoice exceedingly in the divine naturalness amongst each of you. Blessed ones, have courage, the courage that is required to be natural. And when the Divine Naturalness comes to you, you can have greater protection. Let Me give you a warning here. As you begin to feel Divine Naturalness with each other, do not ever let down on your guard. Constantly stand guard. Use, use, use the Fire of Forgiveness and the Wall of Light Protection.

You must be strong enough to make your own application. Go forward and know that the way will open as you make the effort. We could tell you, but do you think you would make your ascension that way? Learn what is best for you. Make your application. Decide for yourself what you wish, where you stand. Call to your I AM Presence, then if you wish to call to Me, or any of the Arisen Host, We will be happy to assist each one of you. Make application first, or else I cannot come to you.

There is one point of the Law which I wish you to understand. An activity of Light does not depend upon places, things, or conditions. To an extent it does depend upon persons, and thus, to the extent that obedience is given by the individual to his own I AM Presence is the Light permitted to expand out to be a blessing to whatever it contacts. Your application will set aside all obstacles and thus every good and perfect thing can be released, regardless of all.

I caution you not to be concerned about your activity. Concern opens you to many things. Instead, become very still, turn to your Presence, and in no uncertain terms call forth the clear direction, and manifestations unbelievable will come forth. One thing that is destructive is the constant indecision which faces mankind. They are bound by their seeming inability to determine upon a single course of action. When you call your Presence into action, if the prompting is not clear, keep right on with your application and the Presence will always clear it for you. Your I AM Presence is not limited in any way. It is better to go ahead wholeheartedly still calling for perfection, than to stand still wavering and going nowhere. Keep active, keep busy, be balanced, and you will find victory after victory coming forth.

It has been My intention for many hundreds and thousands of years to bring about a nation of Arisen Masters. Before that nation can be a nation of Arisen Masters it must be one of masters, and self mastery is the course upon which every sincere I AM student is embarked.

Understand this: The great majority of mankind want this Truth. The only reason they do not take it is because they do not know that which is constructive, but have drifted into fear. The greatest percentage of energy of the individual is in the feeling body, but the mind must be illumined or the Directing Intelligence cannot come through from the Higher Consciousness. That is so much what is needed, and the blessed students who have learned to operate from the Higher Consciousness are the greatest blessing that ever came to the planet. Unfortunately, there are very few, even in the student body, who have applied sufficiently so that they do operate from the Higher Consciousness, which, of course, is one in consciousness with the I AM Presence. However, We rejoice that results so far have been tremendous. Now, however, We enter a new phase and expect far greater results than ever before. It will depend largely on your application, the love you pour forth, and your willingness to look always to your own I AM Presence.

I wish you to come to realize how perfectly natural the Arisen Master is. We are tremendously powerful and We have limitless power at our disposal, but always remember that every Master is but one step above the human and is exactly the same as are other individuals, but the human quality has been removed, and no longer do error or mis-qualification take place.

The unfortunate thing in the minds of humanity is that misunderstanding in the difference between superhuman and supernatural. So many who love to believe in Our reality seem unable to comprehend that We are superhuman and still not supernatural in the least. When mankind comes to understand that, you will find that they will accept Our reality much more quickly.

We are concerned with the safety of America. The safety of this planet depends upon mankind accepting Us. The precious I AM students are the ones, through the power of radiation, who can make this possible.

About 85% of the difficulty that mankind faces is all in the imagination—a sad thing, but indeed a fact. Mankind faces the results of their own imaging, which, of course, is the activity of the imagination. Those imaging faculties could naturally result in manifestations, and that is the deplorable thing. So everywhere today you will observe people, men and women, and even children, turning and sneering at one another, refusing to live by the law of harmony, by the law of love, and the law of reason. Their uncontrolled thoughts and feelings are the result of imagination, or incorrect imaging.

You see how again and again We come back to the original points so vitally important. Before any real progress can be gained anywhere, every individual must definitely govern his own thoughts and feelings, and discipline himself harmoniously in love, that he may express greater and greater mastery through the power of radiation to others with whom he comes in contact. That is the only way. You cannot legislate people to be good. You cannot force the line of action. Every individual everywhere is free and has the God given divine right to expand perfection to the utmost of his ability.

Just be loving and joyous and happy and natural with one another. If you observe imperfection, and of course, imperfection will occur until you make your ascension, just keep on making the call and when imperfection does occur give it no power to act. That is the danger that always creeps in wherever a focus is established in the outer world. There is so much accumulation in the blending of the ones coming together in one focus that unless individuals will move with their face toward the Presence there is little that can be done in building a focus. You will see that as you go on.

I wish to say this to you, and I shall release a definite charge of Light into your feelings so that you will have the conviction necessary for you to know exactly what I mean. I, Saint Germain, am waiting to come forth in My Tangible Body to you, and I will come forth to anyone throughout this planet who will give the necessary obedience. You will hear in the future of various ones throughout the planet who have seen Me and know of My reality. Anyone who will give obedience to the Law of Life does not need to look to another human being to have manifestations from Our Octave! We are unlimited from the Arisen state.

This particular activity will be the freeing and illumining of the individual so that he may be able to stand on his own feet. The activity which is yours is beyond any words of Mine to convey to you. Never in the history of this world have two children been given the opportunity which you have, and the need is great, the Victory of the Light in America stands in the balance, and with what you do will be enough to turn the tide. Do you want to do it?

My activity can never be a religion. I move freely through the people of the Earth. I speak every known language. I speak to Kings. I speak to humble peasants. I speak to Dictators too sometimes, although they do not like it very well. Do you think then, My precious ones, I am limited in that which I do?

In all that you do, be constantly aware that the Law of Being is the Law of Love; it is the Law of Harmony, of Beauty, of Joy, of Perfection. Never criticize nor condemn. If individuals do not agree with what you have to tell them, do not criticize or condemn those individuals. Bless them always and then just go right on, for "I AM"—within those two words lies the fullness of Life.

Never tire of making your affirmations and giving your decrees, and may I charge you to give more affirmations. Many times in the decrees there seems to be the consciousness of asking or beseeching, as was the old activity of prayer, but when you make an I AM affirmation with the full power and know positively that "I AM the fullness of whatever is required," you not only acknowledge the full power of I AM, but you charge it in and through you, and its action is instantaneous. If you will contemplate, as an illustration, the statement of Blessed Jesus: *"I AM the resurrection and the Life,"* you will see clearly how in the I AM Consciousness all becomes one and you move instantly into the realm of Light or instantaneous manifestation always in action. Then, as you are in the realm of Light and become used to instantaneous manifestation, you will observe that with "I AM the resurrection and the Life" you quickly step through the physical world, bringing instantaneous manifestation with you. Also, *"I AM the open door which no man can shut."* I think it would be wise for the students to give that more than they have, for a while, giving those affirmations very powerfully and constantly. Do not let down on those. They are very powerful to your progress.

I assure you, the Power of Divine Love, while it seems soft and is scarcely recognized, still it is mighty and everlasting and sweeps everything before it. Nothing can interfere with it going throughout the Earth to bring its purifying, harmonizing, lasting prosperity.

That does not mean you must love discord or inharmony, but remember, that as an individual maintains life within his body there must be a certain amount of harmony acting, and even though it is almost impossible to observe it, still it is there and can be fanned into a mighty Flame if Divine Love is acting. Even though you contact individuals who are ninety per cent bad and only ten per cent good, still, ignore the ninety per cent and turn your attention to the ten per cent, and ask that it be expanded. It is so magnificent and so real. Do not permit them to talk about destruction. Turn them to something constructive and show them what they can do if they will call to their Presence. Mankind needs that encouragement so much. Magnificent assistance can come forth if they will just obey the simple Laws.

You will find yourself repeating yourself so much, but do not get tired of repeating the same thing over and over again. It is what humanity needs, and if you do nothing more than stand in one place and just pour forth love, still will you be rendering a great service.

Never lose sight of the fact that with every moment you are using energy qualified, even during what we call sleep, and therefore, you are a creator each moment, and what you *think* and *feel*, even for an instant, is a record—it is used energy, and creates.

True, as you know, We have worked through one or two or four or five channels throughout the world, but We are hoping the way will open where We can work through limitless numbers of people, if they will be obedient and loyal to the Light. There are thousands and thousands longing for this Great Truth. So many know that it is real, and yet they have been turned aside by so many powerful things that have crept into the activity.

I assure you there is no limit to what can be accomplished if you go forward in true divine love, for that is the thing man needs. It is not so much knowledge, although that is important, for it must be used to maintain balance, and you know there is nothing that cannot be used if you will apply it in the Name of your Presence; but just to know for the sake of knowing is just to satisfy the human consciousness. It is far better to apply what you know and release it in the Name of Divine Love than to learn too many things. But if you will continue applying, calling your Presence into action, particularly in your affirmations which are so powerful and bring manifestation rapidly, and continue studying the recent Dictations that have been given, you will always find that if your attention goes first to your Presence everything will become the strength of your own power and authority and you will never be led astray in your application or in your studying.

Beloved ones, will you not feel that I am your Friend, your ever present Friend in time of difficulty or in time of great joy, and will you not remember to think of Us at the time of your greatest joy, rather than in difficulty. Then indeed can We sustain all the good that has been accomplished and release limitless power to assist in bringing forth magnificent things. And blessed ones, learn to live as though We were in your rooms with you.

It shall be My great privilege to give you instruction which has never before been given to humanity of Earth.

II

ILLUMINED OBEDIENCE

by Saint Germain

More and more is the consciousness of mankind everywhere being raised to realize that "I AM" is the name of God. Thousands upon thousands of people are feeling this in their feeling worlds, and although they do not understand it, still they are feeling it, for many magnificent people are looking now as never before to the Light. You precious ones must carry that Light. You must do all in your power to get this Truth and this consciousness of the I AM before the people, not only from the feeling standpoint, which your decrees are doing, but from an intellectual standpoint as well. That is from a standpoint of illumination, of God understanding on the part of each individual.

Every individual must be ruled by the heart, but he must have illumined intelligence by which to express the perfection which is required and by which to guide himself into that which is constructive only. Unless one has a clear understanding of the problem involved, and is able, through alertness and balance to follow that clear understanding constructively, even though his intentions may be excellent, still he will make so many errors he can be of little service to the Great White Brotherhood.

It is imperative that each one learn quickly to charge himself with illumined obedience to his I AM Presence. Please, I prompt you, do not have an opinion concerning one another. What each one of you is doing is no one's concern but his own. Each of you will pass through certain phases of expansion of the Light. One day you will find that you have certain things to handle. The next day they will seem to disappear, and the following day there will be something else. This should be of no concern to anyone except the one going through the experience. Your only concern is to call the I AM Presence into action, and know all is well.

It is imperative to learn that in this New Dispensation which I have released *there is no failure,* and those who come to you will be loyal. They have no place else to go. Not loyalty bred of force, but loyalty bred of Love.

Feel yourself at-one with your own God Presence constantly, and then there will be no sense of strain or power of antagonism, but just a calm knowing and calm thinking of that which is correct.

Put aside all thought or feeling of criticism and bring love and harmony, youth and beauty, joy and God Power to the physical octave, then indeed will you raise everyone everywhere into the Oneness of the I AM Presence with yourself.

Charge yourself with the Power of Harmony, the Power of Love in Action, and you can serve as My channel, and those who turn to you will see that it is possible. Be kind and loving; be ever ready to assist, regardless of what you had planned to do. Only by being joyous and loving can I bring mankind into the freedom that is necessary.

In your activity of blessing always, never permit blasting to take place! That does not mean that you cannot defend those material things which are correct. The Light does not need to be defended, but constructive things in the physical octave do need to be defended. Were that not the case it would be the point of wisdom to disband all army and police forces. That will come when that can be done. Until that time, to disband them now would be to cause greater chaos than ever, for unless the individual has learned to govern himself and be the law and order, some sort of order must prevail even though it is a law of force, which We heartily wish did not have to be. Inasmuch as force is necessary at times to hold the rebellious individual upon the pathway of law and order—and remember, law and order is the first law of the universe—then so long must force be used. But your activity is the transcending of that and bringing peace, which will make force unnecessary in the future.

Let Me say one more thing concerning the use of your decrees and affirmations. Do not fall into the mistake of feeling that you must decree by the hour. That is not necessary. I have told you repeatedly that one decree issued with feeling is of much more value than hundreds of decrees issued as a matter of empty form. True, the form is powerful, but a form or a ritual will not save a nation, and who knows better than I, for I am in charge of that activity. Individuals bigger than form, whose daily life is the greatest form of all, a ritual of adoration to the One God, directed by the One God, I AM, is the only thing that can save America. We need strong individuals. We need individuals so strong that they are big enough to love all the time. Remember that, I prompt you.

Light Rays

May I suggest that if you wish more knowledge concerning Light Rays your knowledge will come to you just exactly the same as more knowledge comes to a musician. The musician who wants greater knowledge in music practices more. If you will take the instruction which has been given in the books which I have already mentioned to you, use that instruction. Remember that a ray of light which moves in the physical realm always moves as a result of *thought*, of *feeling*, or of *spoken word*, thought being the activity of the attention, of course. However, in the octaves of Light, in the octave of the I AM Presence, a human feeling does not have the action of the Light Ray.

The Light Ray may proceed on its way instantly upon your call. In other words, it is the same as though there are two actions of the law, but in reality there is only one. As you call the I AM Presence into action to do a specific thing for you, the Presence releases the Light necessary to accomplish the specific thing. You do not feel it until it enters the physical world, and you do not feel it in the physical world until you accept that it moves forth from the Presence. Then as it moves into the physical world, your own thought or feeling, your own desire to give a blessing or to have that which is perfect for you, will clothe that pure Light Ray with the pure energy from the heart of your own Presence with the quality which will produce it. It is that way that precipitation takes place in the physical world; however, may I caution you that when you are nearing the power of instantaneous precipitation, and you are all much closer to it than you know, it is still advisable to continue using the physical objects in the physical world by physical means. You will find, for instance, that it will be possible for you to move one object to another place merely by using the Light Ray, however, there is no necessity of that at the present time. You have been given physical means for doing so, then use physical means. You must fulfill the law of use by being balanced, sane and sensible in all things. All of you could sit still and concentrate on moving a chair, and doubtless you would do it, but of what use would it be, when the tremendous energy could be used to call forth a blessing to others. That tremendous desire for manifestation is what interfered with the Theosophical Society, and that is one reason why I do not come forth in My tangible body any more than I have, because just as sure as that begins, with most there is a tremendous desire for manifestation, and that desire will move individuals into the psychic realm just as sure as there is a sun and stars. That is not what is important. The important thing for the individual's own progress is his own desire to give a blessing to mankind.

In using the Light Rays, if you will use them always to give, you will never lack for any good thing. All of you are a constant action of Light Rays. Every thought, every feeling, even an idle one, is a ray of light which goes forth. Could you see from the inner standpoint you would find you are great flashing beacons of Light constantly, and when your energy is low the Light is very dim and the flashes come as dull glows, and when you are vibrantly charged with energy those flashes go forth as powerful beacons of Light. Visualize a great searchlight pouring from your heart, your head and hands sweeping before you and raising the consciousness of all you contact.

Will each one of you go within yourself and pledge yourself anew to your own I AM Presence. Stand on your feet and say: I WILL! I AM! I DO! and then go forth to accomplish what must be done. You must take a positive stand. Be careful, of course, that it is balanced. Just to be positive is not to be right, but to be positive and right is to be a God Being.

One of the first steps to Mastery is to learn to put all detail in its proper place. So many times you have heard it said that it was imperative for you to give obedience, and from the inner standpoint obedience can only be given to the I AM Presence of each one. In the conduct of your outer affairs however, it is always necessary that a form be created and that form followed so that perfection can come forth. If every individual connected with an industry attempted to run the industry it would be a pathetic situation indeed. That is why the Great Law has always taught individuals the selective, discriminating power whereby one may do one thing and another another, and thus in working together in harmony under direction may bring forth greater and greater miracles than any one of them could do singly. In the Arisen state We operate upon the same principle and it is, in fact, merely the lowering of that principle in the physical octave which permits man to be successful.

Why will not individuals learn to command in the Name of their I AM Presence when it is the simple, the certain road to the permanent victory all require? Will you not accept Our Reality and the Reality of your Great Presence? O such doubt as has been released, such fear, and yet what does it amount to? It is as nothing before the Great Light which We wield, if you will but accept it. We cannot help you unless you accept Our help. We are offering it to you with all the love of Our Hearts, and yet, blessed ones insist on turning away, refusing the help which We can offer. Well, that is their business. We do not command, but their own lifestream will compel them. So many times We could protect an individual or group of individuals, and yet if they refuse Our assistance We cannot force them. The Great Cosmic Law of this planet, of this entire Universe, is now forcing them to make the maximum effort, and things are happening with a rapidity which ten years ago would have seemed greater than human endurance.

We have observed every activity and We have discovered many things. Blessed people of Earth have learned much from Our Radiation. It may seem strange to you that such could be, but actually, in observing the human in the last few years, believe it or not, I have learned a few things Myself! Never has there been such a time on this planet as there is right now. Chaos seems to be the order of the day, and yet as I have told you, from the inner standpoint We are very nearly prepared. All is very, very close to the great unfoldment. Will you not, all of you, remember that no matter what occurs, your own Presence, I AM, is the protecting power for you; and I assure you I will personally assist every one of you in a time of great crisis if you will turn to Me with love. I am unlimited in any way and if you are sincere and will turn to Me in love I can move mountains to protect you. Remember that! And do not permit fear to enter your worlds even in observing the great thing that must be done. You must be joyous and loving and release that joy and love. Then mankind will stand with you to do that which must be done. To fear the thing you must conquer is to give it power. Just go forward filled with great joy and determination, and not only filled with it but releasing it so that others may know that here at last is security, here at last is a firm rock, a foundation upon which they and their country may rest.

In using the Violet Transmuting Flame, remember that you as the human do not use it, for the human cannot create a flame, nor control it. The I AM Presence is the Flame, is the controller, the creator, and the user; therefore, in making the call to the Presence that the Fire of Forgiveness come into action, ask that the Presence sustain that for a fifteen minute period and visualize it as taking its activity of fifteen minutes of time, but it does not have to take you fifteen minutes to visualize that. There is no time or space. Think about that. The Violet Transmuting Flame always springs into action at the lowest possible point where harmonizing is required, and the flame goes upwards always.

In dealing with people, always call forth an action of love before you speak. It will handle so many things. It is not necessary ever, except in great emergencies of a physical nature, to release physical feeling in your speech. That is never necessary. Always call to your I Am Presence that there will be a radiation of love, a feeling of joy and happiness in your words. There is nothing so important that that cannot take place, unless, of course, there may be some outer emergency that has to be met very quickly, but even then you can instantly call to your Presence. It takes so little time, and thus you will be prompted to do the perfect thing. Feel the confidence of your own Mighty Presence, and then move forward, dauntless in the power of your determination, in the power of your own Light in action to assist your fellow man.

Why is it that blessed ones who are so sincere, many times refuse to turn to the source of Light and Wisdom, but instead look to channels. Call to your own I AM Presence, and if your desire is sincere and your heart is right, the way will be open for each one. If the way does not open for you as quickly as you think it should, do not blame another, look within yourself. This is positively the Law of Life. When you release enough love and keep yourself harmonious enough, the way will open for the accomplishment of anything. The I AM Presence, remember, is the Full Power of the Universe and is unlimited in any way.

May I say this also: All of you should learn to begin having greater confidence in one another and begin having confidence in the other by learning to be worthy of that confidence in yourself. This applies to everyone. As you definitely demonstrate to one another that your world is in order, you will clear the way for a feeling of trust and dependability as regards yourself. Remember, and I think this will stand you all in good stead, when you have the inclination to become angry or become over wrought, tense, irritated at some condition or some thing, think how futile that thing is going to be ten years from now, and I think you will have a much easier time in learning to control your feelings. No matter what anyone does to you or says to you, or about you, you should not be touched or disturbed in any way.

Have confidence in yourselves, and I plead with you, never destroy confidence in another. A kind word, a generous act, is worth more than all the criticism in the world. Feel yourself always at one with your own Presence, and pour forth love and blessings without ceasing. Thus I can protect you in any and every activity. Know the I AM Presence in each one is the only, the Supreme Power. Feel yourself enfolded in the arms of your Presence and abide there forever.

III

QUALIFY WITH PERFECTION

by The Master Jesus

My Blessed Children of the I AM Presence:

Again it is My great joy to speak directly to you, to enfold you in the Heart of My Love and to bless you with the radiance of My Light.

How magnificent is this new service which is being released to mankind, and the Power which has been released today upon Earth has surpassed anything We have seen for many hundreds of years. All of mankind whose attention has at all been turned to the constructive way of life will feel considerably the radiance of the God Power, the Cosmic Light in Action, which radiance will be sustained for another forty-eight hours. The apex has been reached and from this time on you will find the going much easier.

The gratitude that We in the Arisen state feel can only be imagined by the humanity of Earth. I have labored so patiently with mankind for so long, I think I know them rather well. Such an accumulation of doubt and fear and disbelief has encased the feelings of mankind. Although their hearts have called to Us, yet with their intellects they have gone right on creating, until there is such a vast accumulation that it has made it impossible for much to be transmuted. The release of this Cosmic Light is the second wave of that dispensation the thousands of I AM students have called for. When the third wave is released, all destruction will cease to be. The second wave will do much to hasten the outpouring of it.

My beloved children of the One God, the Great and wonderful Presence of Life, I AM, I wish to speak to you concerning Love, for it is upon the Ray of Love that My service has been rendered to humanity, and the compassion, the healing, the purifying activity of Love is My own special province; so listen carefully to these words which I give to you and cherish them always.

Blessed, blessed children, do not ever feel that the progress which another may make in any way relieves you so that you do not have to make your own application. That is one of the greatest mistakes man makes today. Many, feeling My Love and knowing that which I am today, lean upon Me and lose their way, and so have to return again and again in physical embodiment. Some of you here in this room knew Me in My previous service.

In your application in this radiant circle in which you have been drawn, will you always be humble, so loving to each other. Never let that human thing rise up amongst you. If you feel that coming, turn on it instantly and call for it to be removed. Do not permit any unkind, hasty words to each other. They are not necessary. When you contact one who is vicious, blessed, blessed ones, when you set yourself to battle that individual you take on his qualities. Instead of battling, call for the Wall of Light protection. Your heart of Divine Love will dissolve all things and your presence and blessing to all will serve to make all wish to stand near you, for such is the way of God, I AM. Look well into your feelings, your desire world, and if you find a desire there that is not constructive, do not hesitate to face it. Say: "I now thrust this undesirable thing forth and it is transmuted in the Fire of Forgiveness." When you learn to do this, indeed your heart will burst with rejoicing.

Think well upon the Oneness of all things, and call for the action of Divine Love to be released through each one of you constantly. Do not condemn or criticize. Divine Love is what the Earth needs. Please do not fall into the error that will make you think Divine Love is not a part of the I AM activity, for it is the primal substance that composes all things. O that the blessed students could understand! Everywhere is the call coming from so many: We want Love. We want understanding. We want happiness. We want Peace.

Precious ones in this sacred circle, I am charging you with some of these qualities, and if you will accept their action and feel My tangible presence among you, you will never be the same from today on. You will find yourself far mightier and be able to face conditions which a few days ago would have left you fearful and trembling.

Remember, O remember, I plead with you, put loyalty to your own God Presence above the loyalty to any other thing. Put love to your own I AM Presence first. All other things are secondary. Remember that, I plead with you, for only in that way will you be strong enough to assist in that which must be done.

I also wish to call to your attention the activity of the law dealing with the power of qualification. This is one subject we have not touched upon a great deal and yet it is one of tremendous importance, and I feel it would be well for Me to bring it again to your attention.

More and more Light is being released to the Earth, not only through your own lifestreams but the Great Cosmic Masters Who are the Lords of Creation for this Universe have released certain qualities of Cosmic Light which are pouring forth to illumine the consciousness of mankind irrespective of their own application. This tremendous outpouring that is taking place and is constantly increasing, will repeatedly make you more keenly aware of what is going on about you. You will become, as time goes on, more and more aware of the forces that are playing about you, and that is why I must again bring up this matter of your power of qualification.

When you in your consciousness, through the activity of your feeling world—which is, of course, a part of your consciousness—become aware of a force acting, be certain that you qualify it with perfection, that you accept it as perfection. Should your attention remain upon it more than a few seconds, be consciously aware of an expansion of Light. I tell you truly when I say that if you will just do this you will set up an automatic protection that acts in your feeling worlds and your consciousness to guard you against the destructive force released by other individuals. Whenever you observe something taking place, qualify it with perfection, that way you send forth only perfection and as a result, that which you send forth will in time manifest in your world.

I plead with you, precious ones, do not be curious any longer as to why certain things act and why you apparently have to go on still solving problems, and why you think your Presence does not answer you as quickly as you would like it to. If you wish to know the answer to those "whys," stop asking the questions and apply the Law. You see, with your attention upon a question your attention is upon a negative condition which is seeking a positive answer. Nonetheless, your attention is upon the negative aspect. Your attention is going to the lack and your continued acknowledgment of that will bring it about. If there is something that you do not understand and you wish to understand it, make one call to your Presence and then dismiss it, and I tell you, the answer will at that moment start on its way to you and you will have it. It is impossible for this law to fail! It is absolute, all powerful, eternal.

Turn to your Presence and call for these things, rather than turning to the outer human to longer continue solving problems, doubting and fearing. Will you not believe Me when I tell you doubt and fear are your enemies—in the things appearing about you—in the things that happen to you from a physical standpoint—doubt and fear are your enemies. Push them aside! Call that they be dissolved and transmuted from your world, and stand free, knowing your Oneness with your Presence, knowing that the Almighty Heart of God is your heart, and that your love is God's Love, your intelligence is God's Intelligence, your life is God's Life. You are then one with your Creator and as such you become the Christ, the Only Begotten Son of God.

You are witnessing a world filled with great changes, changes which are bringing about, through much trial and sorrow, the glorious fulfillment of all the prophecies, the Golden Age. These appearances, which are not comforting, have no power. These changes which seem so mighty and far reaching, so unprecedented, are of small concern when We in the Arisen state consider the magnificence of what will come through them. Again I caution you to keep your attention upon the goal of life, your own I AM Presence, and refuse acceptance to the appearance world, and even when your attention does go to the appearance world, qualify that appearance with Perfection.

You see, dear ones, you have such tremendous power in regard to your qualification, and if you are wise you will qualify everything that happens with Perfection, whether it blesses you or not, still qualify it that way, and thus, with your attention upon Perfection you will be decreeing it into your world.

Be natural and joyous in all things. These great Truths of Life which have been brought to you are natural, joyous activities, and not some painful long drawn out proposition that leads man to the grave, but rather the glorious all enfolding Light which does away with all that old activity and leads man from Light to greater Light—from greater Light to still greater Light, until man becomes all Light and thus returns into himself.

Could you see the perfection that is in store for you, dear ones, you would rejoice exceedingly, even though you knew, as We do, the road that awaits before you. Even though parts of that road may not be bright, still, blessed ones, when We see the goal I assure you We do not mind the journey. Thus it was that the early pioneers in this country managed to struggle across what were then trackless wastes of land and desert, because they knew the end. Will you take My word for the end which I see before Us, which is glorious beyond your most magnificent anticipation? Will you accept My word in this matter and then rejoice and go forward regardless of any difficulty?

Why is it that when My Name is mentioned so many times mankind promptly lose their joy and laughter and they become very serious? They go about almost with fear that I might be displeased. I wonder if they think I am not aware of their wrong doings? I wonder if they think that they fool Me? Precious ones, I am no long faced individual. As a matter of fact, do you know that I had to make many calls Myself to silence gossip concerning Myself, for would you believe it, a group of people began to spread the report during My ministry that I was a drunken fool, given over to much carrousing and much jesting—that I picked My friends from all the derelicts—in fact, that I was not a decent sort of person to have around. Well, precious ones, that is the type of thing that happens so frequently. You know some of that gossip still has come down two thousand years, but it doesn't affect Me. It only affects those who carry on with it. And so it is with you precious ones. If you stand clear of all gossip, the gossip will never hurt you. It will only hurt those who give it forth.

When I think that all those reports concerning Myself began because I wouldn't do what people thought I was going to do it seems most amusing, but naturally, you see they felt that when I went into a synagogue I should go through certain prescribed ritual, that I should become long of face, very doleful, and follow the very ancient and badly inter-preted laws of Moses. And when instead, I walked into a synagogue with a bright step, joyous smile, touching the shoulder of My friend and neighbor, it was too much for them. I have been too much for them ever since, and precious ones, you who stand by the Light are too much for those who do not. Even though there might be only one of you, still, if you are with the Light you are too much for the opposition.

IV

THE LOVE OF AN ARISEN MASTER

by Mighty Victory

Beloved Children of the Light:

My joy and happiness in being with you today is something in which I am sure you do not completely understand. Long have I anticipated this pleasure, for San Francisco and the entire Bay district mean a great deal to Me, of this I can assure you.

For a long time, a very long time, humanity has pulled this way and that, ever taking sides and then either side striving to conquer the other by force, by cunning or by any means at their command. That day shall cease and the Victory of the Light in America shall be made manifest! I Am Victory! For tens of thousands of years I have represented Victory, and My Power is far greater than all the mass of mankind together!

With the coming of this Light and this Activity, the defeat of all viciousness, bewilderment, and doubt of the reality of Saint Germain's work will be complete! The seething mass of human feelings shall go down swiftly and the New Golden Age will be at hand; for the Light, the I AM Presence, is the Full Victory and Power of Light itself and knows no opposite!

How We wish, from the Arisen Masters' standpoint, that the beloved students everywhere would learn to let go humanly, and calling the I AM Presence into action, experience the fullness of all that is waiting to be released. Long have We labored to bring about this condition. Why will not mankind understand that the only reality is Life, their own individualized Presence of Life, whose Name is "I AM."

The progress which must be made depends so largely upon the calls of the students. But I wish to convey to each one of you with the full Power of My Being—do not let down in your application, but keep right on and feel the Full Power of Light sweeping into action with every call you make.

I wonder, do you quite realize how much We love you? I wonder if you quite realize what the love of an Arisen Master means to you yet in the physical octave? That which all the world requires so much is Love. The putting aside of every human thing is the only source of real Love—Love Divine. And yet, I say, I wonder if you quite realize what the Love of an Arisen Master means to each of you?

The Love of an Arisen Master is the fullness of Divine Love, for that Love is the Arisen Master's Consciousness of Love, which is the all powerful, the all enfolding Essence of Life itself. It is the Power that creates. It is the Power that sustains, and in it no human concepts ever act. Do you begin to see what it means to have an Arisen Master say to you: "I love you"? The blessed humanity of Earth is starved for love. What a great pity. And yet, because of the action of the human consciousness and the substance of the human will, individuals fear to release love to their Presence, or to things, or to people, lest that love be misunderstood. Well, perhaps in one sense of the word that is very wise, but in another, think of the great pity that real Love could be misunderstood. How We long for the day when humanity cease to look upon the human and accept their own responsibility and learn to love with the Purity of the Arisen Master.

V

BE NATURAL - BE HAPPY

by Urlando

This evening I am going to take up certain things with you and I am sure we shall have a very good time. You will recall that My activity is one of great joy and for the most part, indeed almost every Arisen Master has a sense of humor. In fact, without that sort of balance, that balance whereby a man may laugh at himself, the ascension is practically impossible from the human standpoint. Remember, I have come through every step of the way just the same as you must do. Even though My Victory was attained in a far off day, still it was not so long ago that all of us stood together in the physical octave, and inasmuch as I have gone ahead of you, consider I have gone ahead to prepare the way for you, and your attention to the I AM Presence, and your application, will bring you to the place that is already prepared. Accept that, will you?

I plead with you, precious ones, be so completely natural at all times. To be completely natural is to be an Arisen Master, and I assure you, We are far more natural than you are. You are actually subnatural, which is a most uncomfortable condition. You really should come where We are, it is delightful, and as you keep making the call, being unconcerned, you will surely find your way to Us.

Here is another point, and it is a great indication of the fact that many times a law, a rule, will have two apparent sides which will appear to be absolutely opposite and yet they will be the same thing. First of all, of course, the arisen state is the goal of mankind and must be accomplished from the physical side by the individual's own application. Every individual if he really wishes the ascension, makes that application with all joy and earnestness, and not just standing still waiting for the ascension to take place.

Precious ones, if you could see what I have observed you would positively be amazed. Blessed students, with the opportunity of a lifetime, stand still and let others take advantage of them, passing up wonderful opportunities because they expect to make the ascension. Please do not fall into that fallacy. That is an erroneous way of thinking—that is absolutely ridiculous. Of course the ascension is the goal, but those who refuse opportunities in the physical world will never make the ascension because the arisen state is attained by rising from the physical by expanding the Light so much that you rise out of it. But that has to be done in action, in joy, in beauty, in happiness, and does not come about by the individual's ceasing to make effort and standing by and saying he wants perfection immediately. If it were as easy as all that you all would be Masters.

As you go forward in this great and wonderful opportunity which is yours, refuse acceptance of appearances. From the appearance world so many things could take place, but they never do, so why be concerned? Do not focus your attention upon appearances. Know always the Power of Light is the only reality, and that Power will sweep into action with the fullness of Itself when you speak in the Name of God, I AM. Go about with certainty, and thus you will move on your way, always protected, always illumined, and you will be great pillars of sustaining force for others of mankind who do not as yet know this Law.

We never intrude upon an individual's free will. We don't have to and We don't do it. An individual who calls to the Presence to destroy another individual, or to bring discord into their world, or to do something destructive or negative, one who makes such a call is using black magic. Use those decrees which have been given to you and realize what they mean to you.

Another thing I would like to call to your attention is the activity of looking for phenomena. My goodness gracious, I tell you I have seen some of the most amazing things among the students. I have seen in hundreds of cases, some individual will do some little thing, meaning to give a blessing to some one, and that one, not observing the individual perform the act will accept it as a manifestation of the Arisen Master. And do you know, rather than tell the truth about it, the one who has performed the little act of kindness would rather cut his tongue out than let on that it was he and not an Arisen Master. And why do you suppose that goes on? Purely from the desire to have manifestations. Don't you see you must be honest with life, and with each other. Don't let anyone think he has a manifestation when it is not, for goodness sakes unburden them! When a manifestation takes place it is an activity of Light and is an Inner activity. Turn your attention to the Inner causation that you may have the joy awaiting you. Why continue to look to the outer world for that causation? You will never find it there. It is on the Inner, and then you have it in your world and you do not have to look outside for it.

Another point which I think needs a little explanation is the matter of energy. You have been taught that the energy you release is either qualified constructively or destructively. It goes forth to perform its service and comes back to you. Now that is absolutely correct, but there is something else in regard to that which you should know. It takes a certain amount of energy released in the physical octave to keep a balance in the physical world. Now that energy is constructively qualified, but it is not necessarily qualified through a decree. You might qualify it by reading a good book; that is energy. It has been released constructively, certainly not destructively if it is a good book. You might release your energy constructively in singing, not necessarily an Arisen Master song, but any song, a good song. You might release your energy constructively by playing a game, by swimming, by hiking, by doing any number of things in the physical octave, and precious ones, those things are necessary if you are to maintain balance in the physical world.

Dear ones, will you remember to follow the Laws of the Arisen Masters, and will you forever challenge the human? Remember, if We give you a Law We do not at the same time give power to an individual to enforce that Law through you.

When humanity will accept that reality which I AM, will

accept that reality which each of the Arisen Masters is, then the joy in their hearts will know no bounds, and at last, standing face to face with your own reality, will go forward with a speed which will amaze you and them. It is magnificent to know the joy of taking your hands off and standing free, blessing all mankind, blessing all activities, and standing free and clear above them, as Master, knowing the beginning and the ending, seeing all things.

Your activity must be an activity of love and blessing always. Bless all individuals who make mistakes, but do not let those errors into your world. Don't see them! Keep your eyes off those mistakes! When you see something taking place that is not right, rise above it and move on. Do you not think that is what We have to do? How patiently We have worked with you. You have made mistakes but have We blamed or criticized you? No, We do not do those things. We see the good, the Light in your wonderful, beautiful hearts. We know that Light and pour to you that Light which is Our own, the consciousness of complete victory, that you may walk hand-in-hand in the beauty and perfection which is yours today.

Do not, I plead with you, try to correct each other. Never, never, never interfere with a human being, because it is such a temptation to try and step in and give advice to another member of the human family. Do not do it! The correction of the individual must come from the individual if he is ever to be free. For you to turn and correct another, instead of making the call for him to correct himself, you not only bind him but bind yourself. In this way you both lose. O yes, it is possible to guide humanity carefully, giving them the Law, explaining the reason why. That is the divine thing to do. Make no decisions for people, make them for yourself, because you are master of your world, but you must not interfere with the world of others.

Learn to work with humanity. Do not be afraid to stand and declare these high ideals. Stand true to them. Do not let the temptations of the outer world take you aside from your sure and certain victory. How humanity loves to wallow in the pigsty. They love to appear to each other as a little bit worse than they really are. Isn't that silly? But they love it, and because they do, that is the condition in which they find themselves. Do not, I plead with you, permit yourself to be attracted, because it just holds back your progress; it slows down the activity and holds back your financial freedom, giving you additional things to handle. Stand free and clear!

So many times apparently sincere students will say: O what I should do is to bless that one . . . or some such thing. They will think the call they ought to make, but will they make it? That is the question. If you will just make it a point to *be* the Law; do not think you ought to love one another, *love* one another. Yours is the course of action, bringing perfection everywhere you move, for perfection is what you are aiming at, perfection first in your own world, and as you find it there, as master, you turn and expand it, for that is the Law of Life itself. *You cannot create perfection if you haven't it in your own world.* Perfection is possible for each and every one of you because you come forth from the perfect source, and nothing but perfection will ever satisfy you.

Sometimes We hear the humanity of earth discussing this matter of perfection and they will say: O how boring it will be when everything is perfect—and of course, that is quite silly for if all were perfection it couldn't be boring. Do not be afraid of improving yourselves; do not be afraid of being the Law, the fulfillment of the Law. O I do not mean now that you should rise above your fellows and lord it over them and say, -see what I have that you do not have,- that is not the Law. Do not be afraid of standing clear and free of human conditions in your world, but, if you wish to make progress never stand aside from an individual in need of help. If you see a child of God dwelling in misery, if you look at the misery and find that it is too terrible to get into, dear ones, you will regret that. You, in your position of advanced students on the pathway take the responsibility of being master, and that means you have divine authority, and there is no individual who cannot receive help from you when he asks for it. You represent a tower of strength, a pillar of Light to him. That you must become.

VI

STEADFASTNESS TO IDEALS

by Saint Germain and The Goddess of Peace

I charge you with all My Arisen Master Consciousness, with My Arisen Master Power of Love in Action, for you must never forget in all that you do that Love is the great molder of the Universe; it is the Great Power of Light in Action; it is the highest rate of vibratory action in the Universe. Love is Light, it is God, and when you are releasing love, whether it goes to your own God Presence, as it should, or to a person or object, you are happy, for it is the outflowing of that love which is a real substance. As I have said, it is Light in Action that makes it possible for happiness to be; therefore, how magnificent when we understand that the outpouring of love in gratitude and adoration to the I AM Presence, the individualized Presence of Life for each one, is the greatest service that can be rendered, is the most magnificent way to attain permanent happiness that there is in the world.

Knowing that should not turn you aside from accomplishment of many things in the outer world, for never in the history of the world has the need for outer accomplishment been so great. Could you see from the unlimited standpoint you would observe that the feeling worlds have become very dark grey in color. There is a tremendous momentum of fear at large and it is particularly for the purpose of protecting yourselves from it that I am come this evening.

It has been said that fear is the only thing that can chain a man. It is not the only thing but it is perhaps the greatest thing. Fear is caused only by a lack of confidence in the Living Presence of the Pure Christ which dwells within you and above you. *I AM that Radiant Christ Self in Action sustained. I AM the Power that controls my feeling world, that harmonizes all things, and that keeps me charged with the feeling of confidence, with the feeling of courage, with the feeling of dominion, (for all those things are feelings). I AM the Presence that puts aside all activity of fear, not only in my world but in the world of all with whom I come in contact. I AM the Presence of confidence charging forth now that mankind may acknowledge these qualities and go forward into the New Golden Age.*

Do not think that just the maintaining of harmony and love for yourselves is sufficient; rather must that harmony and love be released in an unending stream that those who contact it will be drawn into this Sacred Focus which I have established. I say to all those who hear these words or those who may read them, as you hear them or read them turn to your Presence and ask who is giving this forth. Ask Me also if I am real, and your feelings will convey the truth to you.

Remember, in all the things that may be directed against you, either from the inner or the outer, unless you accept them as having power to act in your world, they have no power and will dissolve before the conscious and constant outpouring of Divine Love which you release. Above all, I caution you to watch your feelings. Do not become irritated in the slightest. Maintain a calm, poised, peaceful, loving attitude to one another always. Remember, you are responsible for those things which you do and feel, and know that you have full power to control your feelings. Is it not silly to let some little temporary thing come in and cause you to release great energy misqualified? Silence it instantly!

It matters not what an individual may say or do against you. Stand firm and true to your I AM Presence, and I assure you that your love sent to Me or to others of the Great Ones will always reach us. Affirm: *Peace, be still and know that I AM God, the full Power of Light in Action in my being and world now and forever sustained by the constant expanding flow of Light from the Great Central Sun. I AM the Pure Essence of God Life enfolding me, flowing through me, and raising me into the conscious understanding of all things.*

And now may I introduce to you

THE GREAT GODDESS OF PEACE:

Beloved students of the I AM Presence, beloved children of Earth who today stand facing the destruction of war, the dissolving of governments, the dissolution of all things which have appeared so permanent, hark what I tell you: War and rumor of war shall cease quickly from this planet! Divine Love shall reign supreme and I, Who am the Great Goddess of Peace shall again rule! My Light shall light the way for all mankind. My Peace shall come forth now sustained very quickly and then for the next ten thousand years will Peace reign upon this Earth!

Myself and Others have been working, although apparently forgotten by mankind, to bring about not just a temporary truce but a lasting, a God Peace upon this Earth, and it shall come forth! Prior to that time the struggle will be fierce, but when peace comes forth now all struggle shall cease to be. Although many will lose much and although much has already been lost, still the attainment of peace upon any planet is always worth a great price. With Earth, We deplore that the price has been so great, but We know that because of the great price, that which I bring will be appreciated the more.

I AM PEACE, and My Peace is not a dull sleep, it is not lethargy, a drifting from one activity to another, but rather it is a dynamic, positive, powerful Peace in Action that releases the fullness of all good things to all mankind and causes them to build in love in what is the New Golden Age.

Call to Me! Call to Me as you have never done before, that My Rule may be quickly established and the destruction unleashed shall vanish from this Earth.

Saint Germain continues:

We rejoice exceedingly in all that has been done. You see, My beloved students of Light, the important thing is always the control of your feelings; the control of your mind; the control of your own body, and when We can have a group of students large enough throughout the country who have learned to give obedience to the Great Law in that respect, then We can accomplish miracles, for you see, as We can bring a group together harmoniously, that harmony spreads out in ever wider circles to enfold those with whom it comes in contact. If the circles spread far enough and the group is powerful enough it will ultimately enfold the entire planet. The imperative thing is self control of the individual.

So much has been accomplished. It is so marvelous to realize that all you have to do, even in conditions of extreme disturbance, is to still the body, the mind, the feelings, and call your Presence to release Its energy, realizing it is God in Action working through you to bring about a condition of perfection. It is so simple, so beautiful, and so many of mankind will come to understand that.

In being kind to people, be very certain that you do not let them influence you, even when you are kind to them. So many times, with a feeling of kindness in your heart, you will attempt to give assistance to some one whose feelings are disturbed and in your desire to give them a blessing you will sometimes perhaps take in a little sympathy, which will open you instantly to the destructive activity working in their world. This automatically begins to work in your own world and you have yourself to handle as well as them. In being kind, remember also to be firm. It is no mistake to be firm, nor is it unkind. The greatest love usually comes with the greatest steadfastness to ideals, for love without the real ideals, the real truth of life, is not love at all.

Blessed ones, I plead with you, stand by those ideals of life which I have given to you in previous Dictations, in the Books of My series, and which you will find in other great and worthwhile books and documents. Always remember, the I AM Presence is good. All things which come forth that are good, therefore, have come from the Presence. All things that come forth with a special radiation have come from the Presence of some Master. Thus you will see it is so simple to understand this Mighty Law.

It is so easy and beautiful to behold the Blazing Light Presence of one of Us. It is so simple, and you are all so near such magnificent manifestations. I tell you, nothing is impossible to this group if harmony will be maintained and if you will keep yourselves occupied constructively. Especially when something comes up, call on the Law of Forgiveness when something has gotten into your world. Instantly acknowledge that, call on the Law of Forgiveness, and with your attention to your Presence and things constructive, get busy. It is such a dangerous process to just let the mind get busy and mull over things. How the human loves to do that. It loves to hold in its mind ideas and rotate them, which, mind you, is all right if it is a constructive activity, but most do that with things that should not be given attention.

When you begin to have power, use that power always with greater and greater kindness. Remember, no one who comes to you should ever be just shoved aside because you are too busy or just because, well, they are not so important anyway. Beloved ones, if you serve Me truly you will render your service equally to rich and poor alike, to big and small, to young and old. You will have no favorites, but only serve in love. That does not mean that you are not to use discrimination. Naturally you are to use the greatest discrimination, but blessed ones, I assure you that that is the finest kind of discrimination. Treat all men equally. Be honest and honorable in all things. Never lose patience—always calm and serene.

I wish to remind all of you again that it is not possible for one of you to attain mastery through the application of another. I particularly warn you of that because when you find yourself in a group as lovely as this one is becoming and find yourself among such dear friends who are so kind, it is a very simple matter to turn about and rest the burden upon the one who appears to be strong, and that, I assure you, will hinder everyone of you who even contemplate such an action. You must realize now as never before, that it is imperative for the individual to make his own application and to go forward on his own energy, expanding it always in service to the Light, in service to the highest ideals that can possibly be comprehended, which ideals you know, for We have given them to you many times.

In your study and application there are many, many things which you are to do, and I have given you some instructions concerning it. I wish again to call your attention to the fact that there are many wonderful books which have been written which contain great Truths and which will assist you, if you study them, in arriving at a balanced consciousness. You cannot go forward into Victory, nor can you be a valuable addition to the New Golden Age if you are not balanced. O I plead with you, blessed ones, learn to stand on your own feet! Do not rely upon another!

Now let Me also explain more of the Law concerning that, for I have seen so many who, because they had such a great desire to stand on their own feet they proceed, literally speaking, to kick everybody else out of their own aura. You have your own obligation, and that must be fulfilled. Your application to your own I AM Presence, your sincere calls will be the solution to every problem. The solution will not come forth unless you make your application. However, that does not mean that because one does stand on his own feet and makes his own application that he has the right to refuse assistance to another should the other one need assistance. The only reason for your standing on your own feet and thus becoming strong is that you will become great enough to thus render assistance to others. It is not My desire to raise a group of selfish people, but that the strong will give greater and greater assistance to others that they, through their application, will become strong also. Remember always, the pathway to perfection is not the line of least resistance, but you must make dynamic application and release tremendous energy. Those who serve Me, serve Me most when they do not rely upon Me constantly for direction. If they depended upon Me that much then I would be doing it and I would not need anybody in the outer world to help Me.

Further, if you desire to stand on your own feet and put your own world in order, then certainly you must understand that you cannot put your own world in order until you give freedom to every other individualized consciousness to put his world in order too. This idea that one individual has the right constantly to be concerned about the activity of another will constantly get one into difficulties. You must give freedom if you wish it for yourself.

I wish again to remind you that your safety in any and every situation which may occur depends upon your own feeling world and the extent to which you are able to keep it harmonious and pour forth love. When you are able to do that to a sufficient degree you will be safe in the collapse of buildings, for they could fall about you and you would be untouched. However, if you have not learned to put aside the feeling of panic, fear, and desperation, I prompt you as never before to make tremendous application in that direction. Remember, the Victory of the Light has been won in America, but that does not mean that your application is to cease, nor that you can afford to let inharmony drive in. Stand firm so that which has been won may not be lost!

You have been taught that the ascension is the ultimate state; however, so much stress has been laid upon that point that there are some who, in great ignorance, believe that the simple way to attain the ascension is to continue making dynamic decrees until through some miracle it will come about. That, I assure you, is ridiculous. You will not fit yourself for the Arisen state by shirking your responsibilities in this world, nor can you make progress of a lasting nature by trying to evade the apparent difficulties which confront you at the moment. Knowing the full power of the I AM Presence which beats your heart, how simple it is to put your world into divine order. Knowing the I AM Presence, being the I AM Presence, should make you capable of rendering a far greater service in the physical octave than you could otherwise.

There are far, far too many students who know of the Great Law but who really do not apply it because of the misunderstanding of just what application means. To decree is not enough, for My blessed students, let Me assure you, to understand the Arisen Masters' Law of Life is to understand something that is very practical and which should make each one a better being here and now. The I AM Presence is perfectly capable of determining the moment of the ascension, the location of the ascension, and what the service is to be after the ascension. You will prepare best for the Arisen state by preparing best for the state you are in.

I have observed a great many questions asked concerning the difference between the "Inner" and the "outer." This seems to be a point that should definitely be cleared up. My blessed ones, do you not see that when you have entered into the I AM Consciousness that your own individualized consciousness, the I AM of yourself, expands to include all things, created and uncreated, and thus your consciousness is one with all things. Do you see, therefore, that that is not only the Inner but the outer, since consciousness permeates all things created and uncreated, visible and invisible. Enter into that transcendent state and be at peace.

The question has also been asked many times, "Are the Arisen Masters real?" By "real" is meant, are the Arisen Masters physical? No, We are not physical, but We are real, and because people do not see Us naturally does not remove Us from the universe. They can feel Us, and there are several who have felt Us very definitely quite recently, in a nice way, of course.

I am here tonight in My tangible body. You may say, "Why is it that I do not see you with my eyes?" Because, beloved students, to see is also to comprehend, and the comprehension, or the seeing, is an activity of the feeling body, which takes place in the complete I AM Consciousness which I have mentioned. Dwell upon that and much will be made clear to you.

I plead with you, let us have no more criticism. Let us have no more condemnation, even in the feelings. Those things generate and stir up difficulties, and goodness only knows what the results may be. Stifle those things within yourself as you would tread upon a viper, and never permit yourself to think, feel, or speak inharmoniously to another of God's children.

Do you see, beloved ones, that if you have faith in the Law which I am giving to you, then you will permit the working out of the Law in all cases. When you observe an individual who appears to be making a mistake, your obligation is to pour forth love, to accept only God working in that individual, and to dismiss it. Let the Law do the correcting. If the individual is making a mistake he will discover it in time and correct the error, otherwise the error will correct the individual. Do not be concerned. Dismiss from your consciousness the activities of others. Decide for yourself what you are to do and proceed to do it, pouring forth love and blessings at every step.

VII

CLEARING THE WAY

by Saint Germain

Some time ago the Beloved Arcturus promised that should it be necessary, that Light as of a thousand suns would be released to bathe the Earth in its cosmic glory and proclaim to all men the Great Presence of Life and the Host of Arisen Masters. This activity, although a marvelous and wonderful thing to behold from Our standpoint, would perhaps from the outer standpoint be the most terrible catastrophe that could ever overtake the inhabitants of this planet, for the release of that Cosmic Light is so powerful that it would undoubtedly cause the death of better than 75% of the people on this planet. Furthermore, they would not be able to reembody upon this planet but would have to go to another schoolroom. However, the Great Arcturus told you that if necessary that would be done, but from tomorrow on it will not be necessary, for tonight, My precious children, I tell you that the VICTORY OF THE LIGHT IN AMERICA HAS BEEN WON!

When Beloved Victory arrived upon the Earth at the Royal Teton some few years ago, as you all have read in *Unveiled Mysteries*, a portion of the occult law was set aside, and from that time on various portions of the occult law have been set aside from time to time, the meaning of which should be clear to all good students of Light. The occult law, that law which has bound people into the astral world, not permitting the freedom of mind, the freedom of thought and feeling to expand perfection from the physical side of life, those laws are the things which have created and maintained some of the most destructive things upon this planet, and from tomorrow those things shall cease to be! THE VICTORY OF THE LIGHT IN AMERICA HAS BEEN WON!

The service rendered by the calls of so many sincere students in the clearing away of the astral world over America has been of marvelous assistance, but I assure you that that which has occurred, and will be completed tomorrow, is of even greater assistance than that, for the old laws which have made it possible for individuals to hold dominion over others through mental force of one kind or another, be it good, bad or indifferent, will now be set aside. Only one power, from tomorrow on, will ever be recognized by the majority of mankind, and I tell you to watch this and think what it means, for from tomorrow on mankind in the majority will accept the Power of God as a reality! Do you see why I say – the Victory of the Light in America is won! This Victory of Light will now expand and it will include all men, not as a creed, not as a religion, not as any organization. Watch its action. The brotherhood of man is coming. It is now very near, and those human qualities which have been humanity's way for so long are being replaced by Arisen Master qualities and will make the Golden Age a great reality. True, very quickly you will see some things that will be quite exciting, but the Victory is here and We rejoice indeed as never before.

One of the activities of the New Dispensation is that of learning how to get along with one another by calling to the Presence and the Arisen Masters. I particularly rejoice with those of you who have called to the Great Master the Venetian, and to My Brother, El Serapis Bey, for assistance along those lines. Heretofore very little attention was paid to this activity because of the great focus that had to be built and the great power of Light called forth in those mighty decrees to assist mankind in their feeling world, whether they liked it or not. But this group, if it is to remain as a sustaining power of Light for this hemisphere, perhaps more than this hemisphere, will have to know just how to handle themselves in any and every emergency. One of the most remarkable things about the human consciousness is that the greatest emergency of all always comes about when there is no emergency!

The most difficult thing for the human consciousness to do is to be still. Many times We have stressed to you that it is very imperative that you learn the Law of Silence, the Law of being still, for it is only when you are still that sufficient obedience is given the I AM Presence for Its full power to work through you. Do you think that when either one of Us is rendering a great service that We are moving about? For the most part We are very still, for in the stillness is the great power, and I would suggest that you turn your attention to the Oneness of all things in that great stillness which you enter into.

There will be some who will seem to find great difficulty in arriving at that point of stillness, and they are the ones who always need that activity most. I assure you, blessed ones, no progress can ever be made, that is permanent progress, without the individual first becoming still so that the power can be released that will bring about the progress.

Precious ones, I plead with you, take your attention off appearances. Take your attention off human qualifications. Take your attention off the human of each other. Know that it is only God, the I AM Presence, that acts in each individual always, that there is no exception among individuals. The Power of God, I AM, works through you, through all human beings, through every human consciousness. That is your great privilege and when you really do release that Light you will have very little difficulty in becoming still, or in learning to love your neighbor as yourself.

I wish you to know that We never use a destructive force, and although We may use great force and power, that force is always wielded with Love for the permanent blessing and benefit of mankind. We do not find it necessary to use any destructive force, nor could We if We wished to, but that does not mean that We have to be mollycoddles; and I would advise you precious ones to mold your actions after those who have already attained their Victory. You know of many of My experiences. You know of many of the experiences of the Blessed Godfre, and certainly you are familiar, or should be, with the experiences of your Elder Brother, the Blessed

Jesus. You will find no greater examples. Follow them. Do not ever strive to mold your actions after those of human beings, it does not make any difference how much you love them or how much they love you, put yourself above all others. It is far better for you to make a mistake and learn thereby, than for you to prove one wrong through the advice of another and learn nothing. Learn to live, not for self but for your God self and accept your Oneness with the Great Flame of Life within you. I tell you, if you could even for a few moments completely accept the Oneness with your own God Presence, inside of a few days at the most your world would be in perfect divine order and your problems permanently solved.

Let Me also give you a little information concerning the Violet Transmuting Flame. The Violet Transmuting Flame is the mightiest cleansing, purifying power the Earth has ever known to be put in action in an insincere world! If you go ahead bluntly making mistakes and say, "O well, I can use the Violet Transmuting Flame," that is the greatest mistake in the world. Remember, it is the law and activity of forgiveness. Unless you wish that forgiveness in your heart you will never have it. You have to be sincere—sincere and at one with yourself. Then you will have your results and you will have them much more rapidly than you can imagine.

I have been quite amused at times to hear various ones say, "O you don't have to tell me about that, I know the law." Well, beloved ones, I wish to assure you that when you know the Law you will not have to explain that you know the Law to anyone else, they will know it, and if you are in some difficulty and some one tries to help you and you turn to them and say, "You don't have to tell me that, I know the law," it is a certain indication that you don't, because if you did you would be willing to accept the help that is being given.

Blessed ones, is there anything wrong with being humble before God? I wish to caution you, let no one among you think that he or she has some part of God more than any other, and therefore, who among you is too proud to receive assistance from one who can give it! Remember, you are receiving God's assistance, not human. In the first place, the human is no good, and you know it! Never be too ashamed of the mistake you have made to joyously try to correct it. Is it not marvelous to realize that regardless of what mistakes have been made, or what long series of mistakes through a series of embodiments, you can call the Presence into action, call on the Law of Forgiveness, don't do it any more, and you will be forgiven. The accumulation of an inharmonious existence will be dissolved and you may go forward with your world in perfect order, your feelings in perfect harmony, and your mind at peace.

Blessed ones, you are dealing with the Great Creative Word, and when you say "I AM" you have opened the floodgates which release into your world Light without limit, unless you wilfully strive to pollute that pure and perfect stream.

I would rather have you make one call a day individually and make that call with all your heart, with all your mind, with all your feelings, than to stand for hours and mumble a lot of phrases. That would never do any good nor get anything accomplished either. Real students of life know better, and never do anything unless they are sincere. Sincerity is one-pointedness. When you are one-pointed you are without flaw in that which you are undertaking.

Let that Great Light of which you are a part now expand within you to permanently sever you from all human conditions and consciousness. Know that I AM a part of that Light—that all things are one within you. You alone, the I AM of you, is the ruler, the Supreme Omnipresent God of the Universe. Yours is the responsibility of your world—yours alone. Accept the responsibility in joy and happiness, with your feelings calm and determined, going forward, and I assure you never will you lack for any good thing, and you will find the way opening before you and Arisen Master Friends springing up to stand by your side.

It is tremendously important that you realize fully just what harmony in your world means, for harmony is the Law of Love. And since you are God Beings, beings created in love, your bodies are held together by the action of love and love only. Inharmony is the opposite of love. It is discord and disintegration, and unless harmony is maintained in your physical, mental, and emotional worlds, those worlds very quickly fall apart, decrepitude and old age fill the individual's body, resulting in what you are all familiar with as death.

The intense harmony of peace in your worlds will very quickly bring the mental, the emotional (that is the feeling world), and physical world into a certain vibratory action where the three become one, and with that harmony maintained it is very simple for the individual to raise himself into the Higher Mental Body and thus the ascension, and he becomes the Arisen Master, which so many have been able to do during the progress of this Earth. And yet, in saying "so many" I wish you to realize that actually in point of numbers, compared to the humanity of Earth, extremely few have been able to accomplish the victory. Still, it is possible, and every individual must ultimately make that final attainment. It is the conquering of all human things.

When you call your Presence into action to correct a discordant condition which stands before you, make the call that your own feeling world is harmonious. Never do you release a feeling against the person who is discordant, nor against the discord. Be very careful about this. Make the call to dissolve and transmute the discordant appearance, but leave that dissolving and transmuting to your Presence, and do not try to release a feeling from yourself to handle it. I have seen some very sincere and earnest students who, when they see something discordant you would think they were going to have high blood pressure. They almost blow up. Is that Mastery? It is no wonder they have stirred up enmity. How can they be master if, when they see a spider they scream, or when they see the colors of black and red they faint? Let us be sane and sensible about these things.

Suppose there is some one you do not know personally but you feel you wish to send them a blessing. Call to your Presence, and again call that that energy flow through your own world, because you are the power for the constructive thought and feeling, and fill their world with the blessing. Never hesitate to send forth through your own aura, your own world, those things which are constructive—love, happiness, success, Freedom, Victory. Charge your world with them and send them forth to everyone everywhere. That which you send forth will ultimately return to you amplified a thousand fold. Therefore, will you please have no fear in using the Law, and no fear or hesitancy in calling to your Presence to give a blessing to anyone anywhere at any time.

Now here is where the difficulty seems to creep in. When you have a loved one, an acquaintance, or even a stranger who is saying something, feeling something, doing something which you know is not constructive, then call to your Presence to dissolve and transmute the discord. Let not that dissolving and transmuting pour forth from your feelings, for that will give you more to handle, but call to your Presence to do it, and you go right on pouring forth a blessing to that individual.

Blessed ones, it is such a magnificent privilege which we all have. Do you wonder that I say "We" including Myself? My dear ones, do you not see that My privilege is exactly the same as yours? I am no different than you. I have just gone a little farther that is all. Then I have the same privilege, do I not? And what do you think I do, blessed ones? Do you think that when I look forth into the physical octave and behold a blessed one doing things which I know he will have to pay for sooner or later, do you think that I scream and call that that one be blasted? O certainly not! I just pour forth My Love, but being one with My Own God Presence, I too have the privilege of releasing My energy to assist, should that one in the physical octave experiencing inharmony care to call to Me.

I feel that you are understanding this now better than you have. Will you not please keep this clear in your mind? You have infinite God given authority to call to your I AM Presence for the correction of any condition, be it good, bad or otherwise. You have infinite right to command divine justice for anyone, but you have no right under any circumstances whatsoever to release discordant feeling nor to become upset in any way over any appearance, and if you have to give a blessing to an individual that is your business, that is the entire activity of life, but do not, I plead with you, have those funny little mental quirks that some way or another you are better than anyone else because you happen to know the Law. Blessed ones, if you knew the Law you would never think that for a minute.

I have seen so many sincere blessed ones who really have been trying, but they don't call to their Presence sufficiently. I would say that almost 98% of those who know of their Presence still do not know how to tell the voice of their Presence from their own human desire, because they refuse to sit still long enough and listen. And many of these precious students have the idea that the Presence is some supernatural thing, and it is not, never has been, and never will be! I am not supernatural. Get that out of your heads if you have it there. There is nothing supernatural about Me, nor spooky either! And will you please stop trying to convince anybody else about My Reality. Live My Reality and they will come around to find out how you do it. I know, you find so many people who scoff at the Arisen Masters. Don't give them a chance to do it—just be it! Let them ask the first question. If you will just live this Law which I have given to you, you will have no cause to regret the belief in Me.

You will never in the wide world achieve your own victory by going off in a corner and refusing to take an active part in the physical world, for you have to overcome the problems of the physical world so that you may ascend into the next octave. You will never do it by making decrees, by expecting Me or Blessed Jesus to jerk you up by your boot straps. We wouldn't do it if We could, and We couldn't do it if We would, take it any way you like.

There is no short cut, and we are all extremely fortunate that there is not. You go forward every step of the way and you walk every step of the way yourself. O, I have seen so much discord created in My Name, and it is so silly. I have seen family after family break up, home after home, and for what? Just because some blessed ones feel that in order to love Me they must clear from their worlds everyone who doesn't love Me. That is one of the greatest things that has caused people to hate Me. I assure you I don't bite, and I have never released anything but Love and blessings to everyone. To say that I would do something destructive against any individual is to malign Me and say things against Me which are not true. Feel, precious ones, that I am your Friend, your Friend who, though invisible to you, walks with you and helps you. Feel that you can call on Me. I will not perform a miracle for you, certainly not, but I AM the Light within you which is the miracle performing all things.

VIII

YOUR SACRED TRUST

by K-17

It is upon the practical aspect of the application of this Law that I wish to speak to you this evening, for regardless of the amount of application which you have made, unless you have been willing to apply your learning of these Laws from a practical standpoint there is much which you probably do not fully comprehend.

You recall, of course, the magnificent motto which has been used for so long in the Retreats: *"To Know, to Dare, to Do, and to be Silent,"* and yet I would like to refer to that again and bring it to your attention once more for it seems to Me that insufficient attention is given to that motto.

Blessed ones, I cannot speak to you enough regarding the matter of silence. Precious ones, this which We give to you is a sacred trust. The privilege which We have in coming to you and the privilege which you have in being here to receive this instruction and this Radiation is a sacred trust given you by the highest authority in the Universe, your own Lifestream, your I AM Presence of all Cosmic Space. We who are in a measure one with that Cosmic Reality are privileged to give you the Divine Instruction whereby you can become as We are. That is a privilege which is sacred and is something which you must fully understand from Our standpoint to really be worthy of it.

Blessed ones, may I warn you that just because your heart is good does not mean that all other individuals feel the same as you do. It is a magnificent thing for you as an individual constantly to turn your attention to Perfection and feel that as a result, the Perfection, that Universal Brotherhood of man must come about. The greatest enemies which you face here in America are invisible: greed, avarice, dishonesty, hate, and fear. Those are the great enemies of mankind, and particularly they are the enemies of America, for America stands for the constructive way of life and as such must thrust from her borders those inner enemies of perfection.

Guard your attention. When a thought presents itself to you, examine it, challenge it and dismiss it. No longer try to find out where it comes from. So many times I have observed individuals who are susceptible to a projection. They will try to find out where it comes from. It matters not where a projection comes from! Your business is Perfection. Your business is Life, Love, and Joy. Examine the thoughts that come to you, in perfect balance, then take your attention away from them so that they do not have power to act in your world. As long as you are wondering where the force is from, whether good or bad, you are wandering from your own source. It takes very little energy to control these inner faculties. It takes far less energy to pour forth your God given energy in the correct channel than it does to desecrate it; and remember, you are responsible for whatever you send forth, so in calling to your Presence always call for Perfection.

Think before you speak, and when you do, speak that the wisdom of the I AM Presence flows through you, and not just chatter. But I would rather have you chatter and say nothing than to release feeling against anyone, because, whether you like it or not, these Laws act. Remember what I told you a short while ago. If you will observe the Law of Silence you will be making the way a good deal easier for yourself.

If you wish your world to be tingling with the joy of life and the joy of doing, stand firm and strong in the realization of your I AM Presence and feel that flow through you every moment filling your world with Light and Love and every good and perfect thing. Then feeling that, accepting that and remaining harmonious, ask nothing for yourself except the privilege of being of greater service. Then observe the action.

Rejoice! Let a song of joy be on your lips and then let that song expand through your whole day, filling it with radiant beauty and with happiness. Thus you will fulfill the Law by making yourself a part of it and you will be Master of all things. You will be the Great God Presence, the Mighty I AM, commanding Perfection everywhere.

IX

THE GREAT SPIRITUAL LESSON
by Saint Germain

. As I flash these words of Light before this precious boy, if you will hold your attention firmly upon the ideal to be attained, your own I AM Presence, and become conscious of the fact that I am speaking through the activity of the All Seeing Eye, which is one with the feeling world of each one of you, you also will be able to observe these letters of Light in the same manner that your beloved one does. If you do not seem to accomplish this the first time you try it, be patient, maintain harmony in your feelings, and I assure you that it is possible for you, every one, to receive in exactly the same manner.

Precious ones, may I urge you each one, those of you who are not doing so, to become more active physically. A great deal can be accomplished through you when you are releasing your energy. Now those of you who are already finding yourselves more and more active physically, keep it up! Do not let yourselves fall back into the old human habit of lethargy and unwillingness, but rather feel the God Flame expanding within you; recognize the God Power flowing through you, and then make the call that you spend every moment with some activity. Do not look to others to put you to work. I cannot caution you on that too much, for one of the greatest channels for the destructive force throughout the world is that channel which appears as a lack of initiative on the part of various individuals in all walks of life. So many times individuals who do not understand the activity of calling to their Presence prefer to blame some condition or individual if their progress is blocked, when the truth is they do not care to take the initiative to make the progress and blame it on someone else.

Please know that I see clearly into whatever problems

you may think you have. Please know that I understand fully the temptations which are about you. Please know that I understand fully the projections, the accumulations, and the negative human things which you must rise above, but precious ones, if I let those things affect Me I would not be Master, for you cannot achieve God Perfection unless you claim God Perfection for yourself. You must rise above the human and be the fulfillment of the Law. That is the only way. You will never in the wide world make any startling achievement or go forward in any remarkable degree until you definitely make up your mind that you will take your attention off human limitation. Turn your attention upon that which you wish to accomplish and hold it there, calling to your Presence to bring forth that which you desire.

Do not accept the feeling of lethargy. Do not accept that feeling of delay, the feeling "oh let's put this off until a little later." If you could see in the outer world the tremendous things that have failed to come forth, only because of that tremendous momentum in the minds and feelings of mankind which says: "Well, we are not just sure we should proceed, therefore, we will not proceed." Caution is a marvelous thing, and delay as long as you wish, when you call to your Presence, but once you have a clear definite prompting to go forward, do so if the heavens fall. Do not let anything stop you! If you will obey that simple request you will find your world coming into order with a speed hitherto thought impossible.

Stand guard over these suggestions which come to you in very subtle forms and which whisper to you concerning various ones in your midst. When that prompting comes and you hear that voice whispering to you—"I think so and so,"—you tell it to be still and turn your attention to your Presence. Never wonder as to where that voice came from. There has been more discord, there have been more broken homes upon this planet as a result of just those sinister suggestions than almost any other single cause. Gossip is an outgrowth of that activity, for that is merely repeated sinister suggestion that comes from the sinister force.

When you receive a prompting that a certain thing is about to manifest, if that thing which you receive the prompting about is a blessing of perfection, then make the call that it come forth quickly. If, on the other hand, you receive the prompting that that which you are trying to do is not going to be accomplished, something is standing in the way. Just because you receive the prompting does not mean that it has to manifest. There is no predestination. If you observe that there is a prompting giving you ample warning of certain dangers which are approaching, do not accept them as having power over you, and rejoice that you have received the prompting in time. You remember the old saying: "Forewarned is forearmed." Then when you receive the warning, instantly act upon it. That way you can quickly build up a momentum that will nullify negative suggestions. You must be positive about these things.

And may I caution you, dear ones, you do not ever have to, even for the sake of politeness or for the sake of good fellowship, you do not have to lower yourself by accepting drinks or cigarettes or things of that sort just to be companionable. If you will call to your Presence for the proper thing to say and the proper thing to do you can absolutely stand free from that and you can help others out of that situation. I am not suggesting to you that you become fanatical in any way but I am suggesting to you that you remain true to your own ideals, and these Arisen Master Principles which We have been giving to you should be, if they are not already, your own personal ideals. When they are enough your ideals, you will have much less difficulty in adherring strictly to them.

Just another word of caution: As you value your progress, as you value your position in this Light, do not any longer permit yourself to become irritated over any appearance, I do not care what it is. The great mistake has always been the breaking of the Law of Harmony, the harmony of your own being. Do not, I plead with you, permit it to happen any longer. When some one does something that you do not approve of, remember, your approval was not asked for in the first place. Your approval is probably not even desired, and your attention is definitely in the wrong place if you think that you should become upset because of the action, the thought, the feeling or the spoken word of another.

Your business with others of God's children is to pour forth divine love and that alone. Naturally you are to be friendly, joyful, interested in what they are doing, helpful in every way, cooperative, willing always to work twice as hard as the rest, but there your responsibility toward your feelings ceases. Of course, that is the greatest responsibility that you could have. Why take on for your world things that you do not need and that will only bring you unhappiness.

Several of you have called that I speak to you concerning cleanliness, and I wish to say this: Precious ones, the Light from the Arisen Master's octave, although very powerful, comes to you like the fragrance of the lily. It is a very delicate, beautiful, wonderful activity. If you wish the effect of that Light in your body you must learn to keep it clean inside and out. You should learn to keep your clothes immaculate. You should learn to be absolutely tidy about all your affairs, keeping everything neat and clean, for dear ones, you have perhaps heard the statement that "cleanliness is next to Godliness," and I assure you that it is. You must be pure and clean inwardly and outwardly if you wish to receive the full assistance which We are giving. Take time to make yourself fit for the Presence of the Gods if you would have them among you. Accept your own God dominion and know that the Presence of the Living Christ is within you. Then do not defile that Presence of the Pure Christ by anything less than a clean and spotless temple. Your bodies are the Temples of the Most High Living God. They are your most precious possessions, for in them you dwell. They are your homes. Treat them as you should. Be joyous and dignified. Be beautiful, and accept your divine responsibility in giving this Light to others.

*   *   *

Your own feeling is the important thing in the giving of decrees, because, do you not see, *your own feeling is God's energy*, the same energy that will be used to fulfill those decrees. It is already in your feeling world. Then, in making the call, if your energy is vibrant, alive, happy, then blessed ones, you will have little difficulty in bringing your decrees into manifestation. If, on the other hand, there is a tendency to be a little slow sometimes, the action is not nearly so rapid in its manifestation; but if you wish to have an example of the other side, if you give a decree too rapidly, even though joyous and happy, it is just an activity which skims over the surface and it will never manifest in the world.

If you will remember that the Presence works through you as an individual, that your feelings are the important thing, and that the quality held in your feeling is the quality that will be released to bring about that fulfillment of your decrees, then you will quickly see how imperative it is that you maintain harmony in your feelings and release your decrees with joy, happiness, and sufficient energy.

Feel yourself at-one with your own I AM Presence. Turn your attention there into that Great Realm of Light. Let your consciousness be bathed in its mighty outpouring of Love and splendor and joy. Look ever upward and onward. Never permit yourself to accept for a moment any human discord or limitation. It has no power to act in your world if you refuse acceptance of it. Be determined that you will refuse acceptance from this moment of any discordant thing.

No longer question, dear ones. No longer doubt and fear. Those feelings and activities will take you nowhere. Rejoice and know in your heart the Oneness of all things. Accept the Substance which We are pouring forth to you and go forward with a song on your lips and love in your heart for all mankind. Thus will you prove worthy of the trust which We, the Arisen Masters, give you, and you will be able to assist even in greater measure than you know in bringing about the fulfillment of the New Golden Age.

Dear ones, in overcoming fear, when you call to your Presence to take fear from your world, then after you have made the call if you will go forward, even though you may still say to yourself that you are horribly fearful of what may transpire, you have proved by your own actions that the fear is a lie and that you as the God Commanding Intelligence can conquer all things!

I say to you that those who have ever felt fear in the application of these laws or in the face of any human problem and have still gone ahead to apply themselves and to move perfectly in the face of difficulty, I say to you, you are far more privileged than those who apparently never know fear, for it is not so much the being courageous when there is no fear that counts as it is the going ahead and doing because you believe in your Presence and have faith and courage from on high even though the whole world shouts at you so that you tremble.

So also is it with doubt. When you go forward and continue calling to your I AM Presence whether doubt acts in your world or not, then you are doing the one thing which proves that you, the God Intelligence, is in command of your activity and whether doubt acts or not, you, the God Presence, commands all; therefore, the doubt or fear has no power and you as the I AM Presence in action in the physical octave move forward to set your world into divine order.

My blessed children, the pathway to the Arisen Masters' octave is no bed of roses, as perhaps you have found out, but is it not glorious to know you cannot fail! Since you have begun you must succeed—there is no turning back or turning aside permanently, for these great Laws you have learned you will know and recognize in all ages to come. You cannot forget them, for they have been released into your consciousness with the accompanying Cosmic Light, with the Arisen Master's Consciousness, and therefore can never be requalified by the human. These Laws and the application you have gained will never leave you, and even though sometimes all looks dark, still you are, now and forever, I AM! *There is no failure for any one of you at any time!*

Do you think these things which I tell you are not real and true? Though they are not physical, they are far more real than any physical thing. O My precious children, do you not see that all physical things have beginning and end—they are a prey to every disturbing element, to every destructive force—but from the inner standpoint do you see the difference? There, there is no change, for all is just eternal Light, eternal One, and you as the "I AM that I AM" are one with your own Source. This is the true spiritual lesson for mankind to receive. This is the great point, the great Truth, and as you make your own Great Command, face your own I AM Presence, and call It into action without fear, without doubt, so will you quickly go forward to gain your victory.

No longer permit yourself to become disturbed in the feeling world by some trivial thing which has no power to act, until you, with a misqualified feeling, pour forth energy and take it into your world, and then you yell for help and say, "O dear, how could this happen to me?" Precious ones, do you not see, will you not believe Me when I tell you that these forces which play at large throughout the world will have no power to act in your world as long as you are free from self seeking, as long as you control your mental and feeling worlds and seek to pour forth love.

O blessed ones, will you not see that this activity which may seem a little strange to you at first, is so natural and real. There is nothing at all astonishing in these words coming forth through the consciousness of another than the one in whom the words are formed originally. My blessed children, do you realize what your consciousness is? Do you understand the mighty power that lies for the most part dormant in your consciousness? Do you realize that *you are your consciousness,* that is, your awareness is yourself, and that awareness of self is your Presence, your own God Flame, the source of all things, and *you are that I AM Presence at all times.*

When the full realization of your own I AM Presence and of these Great Laws comes to you, you will have no difficulty in holding control over your feelings, and you can go forward into your Great Victory in such a short time! True, you blessed ones who have come together in this Focus have come with a pledge upon your lips that you will stand by and see that the Light does not perish from the Earth. That pledge has been on your lips. Has it been in your hearts? Do you wish to serve Me, dear ones, or do you wish to serve yourself? I warn you that if there is a selfish motive you would be wise to call that it be removed.

You must realize that these laws which I give you are given you for your benefit. You do not have to obey them. I will never command it, and I will remain your true Friend whether you obey these laws or not. I have seen the action and the difficulties which you have gotten in, embodiment after embodiment, because you have not obeyed these laws but have preferred to exercise free will against these laws. You must have free will, and you must obey these laws because you want to obey them and not because I say they are the law. Do not obey simply because I use the word "obey." Do not fall into that concept.

If you want the Light with all your heart, then your progress is certain and you will leap forward to attain any goal. Or, are you not concerned with your own position in regard to the Light? If so, you will have difficulty in maintaining your position. So do you not see, dear ones, how absolutely accurate these laws are and how, when they are given simple obedience your world will quickly come into divine order?

X

HARMONY—THE GREAT LAW OF LIFE

by Saint Germain and God Meru

The imperative thing in the world today is absolute honesty in regard to life. People everywhere think that they are fooling life, but that is not possible. Life cannot be fooled. Your own Presence is never mistaken for it is the Complete Perfection from whence cometh all things Perfect. Mankind unenlightened like to feel that they are putting something over on somebody or something, and most of humanity seem to have the idea that they can fool life and get away with it. To those who understand the Law, of course, that is utterly ridiculous, but in dealing with people who do not as yet understand the Law, remember this quality may be acting, and stand guard that the quality does not act in your world. As you value your progress be honest with life.

Now let us be balanced about this matter too. Just because you see there is some little error that has crept into your world does not mean you should brag about it just to prove you are able to rise above a mistake. No, precious ones. Acknowledge that to your Presence and do not tell anyone else. Call on the Law of Forgiveness and then go forward as you have been instructed. You see, dear ones, the human loves to receive attention. The human consciousness of the individual is a mass of desire, and until that desire has been raised by the activity of the Violet Transmuting Flame and the attention held upon the Light, into a place where the desire world is firmly secured upon Light, until that time in the progress of the individual the human things are bound to act.

These activities of doubt and fear which begin as such subtle things, innocent questionings, wonderings, concern, curiosity, things of that sort, lead onward until they become doubt and fear, and are a powerful activity. Think how marvelous it will be when mankind at large has freed itself from these destructive forces. Stand guard over your feelings! Stand guard over your thoughts! Command your physical body to give you obedience, and then with your feelings filled with joy and happiness, go forward pouring forth love to all.

GOD MERU speaks:

There are quite a number who, when they really begin to comprehend the majesty and power of these Mighty Laws will begin making application which will take them forward almost with the speed of Light. Never be impatient with your progress. Though you know with certainty that your I AM Presence is the instantaneous fulfillment of your every call, you also know that with the conditions in the world today it is necessary to establish a momentum in most of the calls that you make before the fulfillment of the call is reached. That may not seem like instantaneous activity, but I assure you, if you will accept the instantaneous quality of Light as being one with your Presence you will rapidly gain a momentum which will quickly outpicture.

It is true, dear ones, and never forget it, that as long as an activity must take place in the outer world there is bound to be a certain amount of imperfection which registers in the activity. It is only the Light, the Spirit, or the Life which is pure and perfect. You as a student, therefore, should always seek that Light and recognize it wherever you find it. *You will find no perfect individual in physical embodiment until you find the perfect Christ enthroned in your own heart.* Then you will find that imperfection and physical shortcomings will have passed from your world.

The greatest danger to any activity of Light—and this has been observed for many hundreds of years—has always been the fear that creeps into the individual or individuals conducting such an activity that they will be unable to supply themselves by calling to God alone. This feeling of fear causes individuals to become quite cunning and very subtle many times in their suggestions to others that the Light must be supported financially. I ask you to watch with Me and with

Saint Germain, and should you find that the desire for money grows greater than the desire to release that money into the service of the Light, will you call to Me or to Saint Germain.

Discipline of the outer self is imperative, and then with the attention held upon the I AM Presence, the Source of all good, and the desire, the feeling, turned in the same direction, you as an individual will become one pointed in your activity and you will no longer be able to make a serious mistake.

Those who find it difficult to remove doubt and fear from their consciousness should understand that the doubt and fear are always caused by a lack of faith in the Presence. You must put your confidence where it can never be misplaced. That is, of course, upon the Great Presence of Life.

There is only one Light, one Christ, one God. That one is "I AM" and with that I AM you are all one. This is the beginning, the ending, and all between.

Saint Germain continues:

As the individualized Flame of Light you must realize that you have all power, so you can command your world to come into order with the speed of Light. Sometimes it does take dynamic application on your part, and you have to determine with every fiber of your being, with every atom that you possess, to command peace and harmony in your world, but dear ones, if you determine to do it you can do it, and when you have done it the victory and the glory and the joy are yours. Is it not worth while?

You cannot make permanent progress in the Light, or for that matter you cannot make progress in anything, until you have at least in measure learned to govern your feeling world, your mental world, and your physical world. You have possibly observed the trained athlete, the individual who has learned through the power of exercise and constant practice, to control the muscles in the body to such an extent that the individual is able to do what to many would seem to be quite remarkable feats, because his body has been disciplined and trained to follow the dictates of his own direction. Would you believe it, dear ones, that there are very few people in physical embodiment today who have mastered their mental world even to the extent that the athlete has mastered his physical world! Because for the most part individuals persist in not taking control of their feelings and they persist in letting uncurbed passion pour forth from them, and then they wonder why they are unhappy and have discord, loss and failure.

You will suffer every experience of inharmony, discord and limitation until you have learned the great Law of Life is Harmony. And the constant sin against the Great Spirit of Life, the I AM Presence, the Holy Ghost, the I AM of you, is the same in which you as a God commanding Presence turn aside from your own harmony, from your own natural expression of perfection and release a feeling qualified destructively. It does not make any difference what suggestions are made to you in regard to the misqualification of energy. You yourself are the commander of your own world and, therefore, you yourself are wholly and totally responsible for what exists in your own world. *You cannot make progress until you maintain harmony in your feeling world!*

Dear ones, so that you do not condemn yourselves and begin to think that perhaps you can never reach such a high state of perfection as that which I have explained, may I point out this: You do have the perfect right to command Divine Justice for your lifestream, as well as you have the perfect right to command love and perfection, joy and happiness into the world of another. This may seem as though you are interfering with the God given free will of the other, but I assure you the God given free will is always seeking love, Light, perfection, joy and happiness; therefore, when you make the call to release those qualities into the feeling world of another you are standing at-one with your Presence and have every right to stand in that way.

Now may I suggest that when you make the call to assist another individual out of a limitation, appearance or condition you remember to use these words of "love, and joy, and happiness," because if you go about with a chip on your shoulder, feeling that someone else is making a mistake, no matter how many they may make, your calls for perfection for the other individual will largely be requalified by your own human thoughts and feelings. These feelings will pour forth from you and charge into the feelings of the one you are trying to assist, and the two of you have ten times more to handle than you would have had singly. Remember, when you call to the Presence you open the way for the Light to flood forth, so do not misqualify your consciousness or your own thoughts and feelings.

Bear in mind that this activity which we are speaking of is an activity of all Life and you cannot trifle with it and come off unscathed. These things are Law and you are responsible each moment each day for what you send forth. What you take into your world you have to handle. If it is in your world you will have to handle it; therefore, *use, use, use* the protection which has been explained to you! *Use, use, use* the activity of the Fire of Forgiveness, and call with your whole heart and soul that you will maintain harmony in your feelings, that perfection can flow forth in your world.

The Great Cosmic Beings, the Legion of Light, are all calling to raise the consciousness of mankind until that human consciousness disappears and the I AM, the God Consciousness, rules supreme.

Be master over your own world! Put aside these silly, trivial, temporary, petty human things! They are of no moment whatever! Turn your attention to the Great Presence of Life, the Mighty I AM, and call for Its action about you. Accept Its full Power in and through you, and stand by that Great Presence with all that you have and are! This is the solution, not only for yourselves but the whole human race. Upon you depends much that must come forth.

Your concern is only as great as your own desire for Light. Then if that is true, will you please pour out Love to one another? Will you not look to that Light within each one? O it makes no difference what has ever occurred in the past or what may occur inside of five minutes. I tell you it makes no difference! Every physical act is only the outpicturing of something else and a physical act has no power! True, you may say, "Well, since the physical act is the outpicturing of something else then we should consider the something else, and if the act is no good then we should get busy and work on this." That is true, dear ones, but let Me show you this subtle way. That is, the Law is not subtle but the human consciousness tries in its subtle way to confuse you. You may observe imperfection acting in some one, therefore you are positively assured that some discord or imperfection is working since it is outpicturing. If you hold in your consciousness the thought of that imperfection, whether it is manifesting outwardly or inwardly, you give power to that imperfection and by your own energy you sustain it in the world of another, even when the other has called on the Law of Forgiveness for it.

You cannot escape this Great Law for you create each moment, and what is held in your attention becomes a part of you, for your life is pouring into it. This does not mean now that you are to shut your eyes and say everything is perfection, everything is fine. Certainly not! But if you will take the stand and insist on perfection in your own world you will radiate that perfection into the world of others and thus you can assist them far more powerfully and permanently than if you insist on seeing the imperfection. What you think and feel you bring into being. If you think and feel perfection you send it forth. If when you observe imperfection in another individual, if you will hold your thought to perfection and release your love and your own power of perfection into the world of the other, you will render a service you little dream possible.

My Blessed Brother Jesus has always been an outstanding example for mankind to follow in the pouring forth of perfection. That is how those who were ill were healed, for when the leper came to Him He did not say: "O my, see this poor fellow here is full of leprosy which was caused by this which was caused by that. . . ." Instead He saw Perfection. He recognized the purity of the God Flame of the other individual and the leper was made clean and pure. You must realize *your obligation to life is to see perfection, to feel perfection, and to be perfection.*

Do not condemn yourself. When you condemn yourself you are criticizing God, I AM, and that cannot be a failure. You cannot use the name of your own Presence, or thought of your own Presence, or feeling of your own Presence untruthfully without untruthful results. Do not do that, I plead with you. If you see there has been a mistake say, "I AM Presence I rejoice I have found this mistake. I see where I have been incorrect, therefore, I AM the Presence correcting this thing." Do not be too proud to say "thank you Presence for this Light and this Love which has come to me."

Rejoice! Let a feeling of love and happiness flow from your heart at all times. It makes no difference what anyone else may say. *You will never rise out of the physical octave as long as you are concerned humanly with humanity.* I tell you, dear ones, I have observed the reactions and actions of human beings from My standpoint for a good many years and I think I know a little bit about it. You do not have to believe Me, blessed ones, but if you do believe, you are the one who benefits. And please call to your Presence that your human desires be dissolved. Seek only the Kingdom of Light and Truth that the Mighty God Flame may expand within you, that you may be the outpicturing of God's desire. Say many times: *"Let Thy Will, O Beloved I AM Presence, not mine, be done."*

Accept now your own Crown of Attainment. Feel that glorious Stream of Life flowing through you without any limitation whatsoever. Take your Scepter of Dominion in your hand and proclaim to the entire world: I AM the King! Then indeed will that Christ child which is born in your heart grow quickly to full stature and you will be the arisen Lord of Light, of Life, and of Love for all mankind.

Here in America We take Our stand, and to this land of Light shall those seeking Light return. Here shall be raised up the new nation, a Nation of God, of Love, and Light. Not without great trials and tribulation will this be done, but the victory is in sight and I say to you who hear My Voice—you have a part to play in this! Determine now that you shall be found worthy. Determine now that you shall put aside all doubts and fears. Determine now that you shall become the worthy channel for the Living Host of Light, and *be* the Law to yourself and to your fellow man!

This is a sacred hour, for We stand upon the threshold of eternity. Long years ago your Beloved Friend and Benefactor (Jesus) came to you and guided you so that never since that time has man been able to forget. Men have laughed and have scoffed and have disbelieved, but regardless of all the laughter and scoffing and the disbelieving, the Truths which have been taught are still the Truth, and these Truths shall now be taught with all the accumulation of creed, with all the accumulation of misinterpretation removed!

I say to you tonight: *You are free!* I free you of all human creation which has filled your worlds, which has made you fearful, which has caused you to tremble, which has made you uncertain! You are free from all those things, and you will feel greater freedom by taking now your Scepter of Dominion, stand forth, and say to that Great Presence: *"I AM One with Thee."*

America

This country came forth in the beginning, dear ones, and Saint Germain and I have both worked to see that here would be a land of Light, a land of protection for humanity of this Earth. This land was raised and purified for the purpose for which it is supposed to be in use now. Make your calls for the protection of America. The sons and daughters of this blessed land must stand together to protect America, for America, standing as high as she does, has only the Light to defend her. (Nada)

You who live here in America are being given the last opportunity upon this planet—the last opportunity to get yourselves ready in order that these human things—doubt, fear, envy, criticism, jealousy, condemnation—that all of these things may be dissolved from your worlds and you may go forward into the New Golden Age. You in America are receiving this last opportunity, and We Who are working at the Inner levels to assist you will give you every possible opportunity, you may be certain. We will give you every possible moment of time which can conceivably be allotted you, but the Cosmic Hour has struck, blessed ones, and the forward progress of mankind is either in peace and love, or in direst darkness and hate. It is up to you to decide where you shall stand!

In your private work, make the calls for divine justice to be rendered by capital and labor. Make the calls that those individuals fomenting strikes and discordant activities of all kinds, be held in abeyance so that the perfection of the I AM Presence can be released and the victory of unification of the hearts and minds of America can be brought about. All appearance to the contrary, humanity as it stands today is closer to the understanding of itself than it has ever been upon this planet. It is true that never before has it quite realized as keenly as it realizes today the difficulties it faces, but at the same time, the fact that recognition of those difficulties is present brings to the consciousness of mankind at large the inescapable fact that humanity must live with itself or perish!

And so, little by little, surely the Light is gaining its supremacy. Little by little hearts and minds of mankind are being raised and purified to a place where they recognize, individually and collectively, the importance of working together and to do away with discord and inharmony. Surely more and more is the realization going forth that what you do to another returns to the doer—that you cannot injure one member of humanity without in some slight respect injuring all. This consciousness is sweeping the planet, and the urge in so many is now an urge governed by tolerance; a desire for justice; a desire for peace, and a desire for understanding. These things are coming about.

The opportunity of service today is world wide. The things that must be accomplished are tremendous in scope, and only when you have the fullness of the knowledge of the Presence of Life and the reality of that Presence can you fully move forward into the complexities which confront you in this age; therefore, do you not see you must be Masters to accomplish these things. Only those individuals who have learned these laws will be capable of a full, unbiased, just relationship in the future.

The time has come when earthshaking things are necessary for this planet! The dangers to humanity are increasing almost hourly. Civilization itself stands upon a brink, as you know, and only education, understanding, tolerance, love, and peace can move mankind from this disaster and let them face the future with renewed courage, understanding, and hope.

As you turn to your Presence and look to that Presence for your leadership and the guidance, which comes right from the heart of the Great Central Sun—and there is nothing finer, more permanent—as you learn to accept it as a fact, practice it in every day life, not as something which has to be approached in church as a religion, but which is just as necessary as your breathing, then you will attain the confidence and the power of your own Presence that will carry you through every difficulty into victory after victory. Tonight I am charging that feeling into your world that you will recognize yourself as the Victorious, the Conquering Presence of the Most High Living God; that you are beings of Light, and that you manipulate this Light according to the dictates of your Presence. Accept that feeling and be the Gods which you are!

XI

YOU ARE THE CHRIST

by The Master Jesus

Dear ones, how My Love flows out to you when I realize that tonight you stand in much the same position as I stood with My disciples some years ago. It is a marvelous thing that in spite of all the discord, all the visciousness, all the human desire, the human cunning, the lust, envy, greed, and avarice, the Light of God has not perished from the planet, and because of your sincere determination; because of your willingness to give of yourselves, that Light shall go on.

Beloved ones, I know many times you have cried out almost in the darkness of fear, saying "My God, My God, is it worth while to keep on when I cannot see my way clear?" and yet you have continued, for your hearts knew the great reality that is here. My precious children, follow those hearts, for when your heart is filled with divine love you never will go far astray. O listen to that inner voice of love and wisdom which always prompts you to do the perfect thing. Listen to it, precious ones, and give obedience to it. Seek not to glorify yourself—seek only to glorify your Heavenly Father, the I AM Presence within you. Surely you know now that *you are the Father.* As you turn your attention to any particular place you are there, and you become that upon which your attention is focused. Therefore, with your attention upon the Father you do become the Father, and the Son, the I AM that I AM, the whole I, One.

Blessed ones, give no heed to the criticisms of those who doubt or fear you. They are also blessed children upon the pathway like yourselves. Only pour forth your love and know that so long as you are true to yourself you cannot—*you cannot,* I repeat—ever fail! Be true to yourself, be perfect— perfect love, perfect joy, perfect tolerance, perfect under- standing. Be perfect by letting the full power of your Presence flow forth to outpicture in the octave where you serve.

As you go into the inner realms of Light during your sleep, I shall endeavor to show you more concerning the activities of wielding the Light Rays, as it is possible to wield the Light Rays only by using the silent thought and feeling, so that you will arrive at that place where you will be able to wield limitless power without ever speaking a word. At the present time it is necessary to use words, but choose them well. Before speaking, call to your Presence first, that they carry a radiation of love and happiness forever.

In this year you see the outpicturing of man's attention upon My crucifixion, but in the year ahead do you know what you will see? You will see the outpicturing of your attention upon the ascension, and you will become aware that life is eternal, that you are that life, and that you go on and on, ever raising yourself by the power of your own love poured forth until you stand at-one with your own Divinity, and accepting it, become the causation of all future events in your world.

I tell you, dear ones, there is no death. Do not be concerned over the temporary appearance which tells you that some one has passed from your midst. You know in your hearts that there is no separation, for are you not all the children of the one God, the Great Light that fills Infinity. How can you be separated? Precious ones, the real separation comes when you go forth into embodiment, if you but knew the truth. Then if ever We could feel sadness, We in the Arisen state might be inclined to mourn, when We behold the great Cosmic Law of retribution demands the return of even an advanced individual to physical embodiment until atonement, or at-one-ment, may be made.

Precious ones, will you not accept your own Sonship, your own Messiahship? *You are the Christ,* as you accept it and dwell therein. Then since you are that Christ, and I assure you none other can be it for you, why not retain your consciousness at that level, rather than lowering it always into doubts and fears? When you as an individual doubt and fear you crucify yourself needlessly upon the cross of human creation. Why do it when the boundless octaves of Light are open to you and you can, with a single bound, leap into them and there remain at peace and happiness forever.

O precious ones, never cease pouring forth love and gratitude to those who have assisted you upon the pathway. Be grateful for all that has been that is good. Sever connections with all that has been that does not measure up to your standard of perfection, and then go on, ever calling for greater perfection that yours may be a beautiful garden of Love and Light.

The conception of various individuals who did not know Me but who heard of Me because of My ministry, has often been one of weakness and sorrow and they have pictured Me as a man of many tears, of great tribulation, and almost utter despair. Those who knew Me best knew that there is no despair in pouring forth Love; that there is no sorrow in a tear that springs from an overfull heart of joy; that there is no tribulation in humbly kneeling before the least of all mankind that the indication could be clearly given of the Divinity and the reality of God the Father.

Precious ones, when you wish to know real joy, seek those who require joy that you may give it unto them. When you wish to prove yourself worthy of the Arisen Host, take that which is dearest to you and give it away. When you wish to rise into the arms of your Presence, do not publicize the fact, and do not hide it. Open your arms and your heart to your own God self and glorify thou that Great Light. You do not have to be ashamed of worshiping Truth, although the consciousness of man has for so long ridiculed spiritual things for they have thought it indicated weakness, just as they thought that My ministry indicated weakness. Yet I say to all those doubters and fearers: Where is your strength? Can you stand forth when you are accused and with your feelings calm refuse to use the power which you have to free yourself? Are you strong enough for that? When some one comes to you and accuses you of that which you know that you have not done, where is your strength that you can stand peacefully and pour forth love, raising the other from the misunderstanding? When some approach to beat you, where is your strength that you do not lift your hand against them but rather call to the Great Presence of Life to bless them always. Do you think that that is weakness, or do you think that that is strength?

While it is true, My precious ones, that in the world as you find it today there are subtle sinister forces that would take advantage of you if you refuse to fight the devil with his own weapons, for they would take advantage of the fact that you would not strike them by cutting you down without a chance, but what have you lost? When you stand for that which is eternal and true you cannot lose. O it is true that many said that I had failed, for those which I taught apparently as long as I was there to teach them from the physical standpoint did not go very far, and in a very short time My enemies overwhelmed Me, from the physical standpoint. And yet, there is no one today who would say that I had failed. You see, that which I tried to do was not to elevate Myself but rather to elevate My God. Did I not succeed? Is not that the great teaching of all life, that you as an individual are no greater than the thing for which you stand, and if you stand for perfection, for the true divinity in man, even though you fall, that for which you stand will go on. Then have you fallen?

Do you see, precious ones, that with this Great Truth you cannot fail! O the difficulty has been that mankind will not believe this Truth and will not act upon it. Rather they always find excuses as to how they should not act upon it, but I tell you, you cannot overdo the pouring forth of Divine Love. You cannot overdo holding your feelings in harmony and joy. You cannot overdo the love you pour forth to your Presence!

Yet these things are not to be entered into lightly. You must approach the task of disciplining yourself in all seriousness, even while you remain joyous in your feelings, for you must study deeply yourself, and look at yourself honestly. You are your own greatest problem, for you as the human self are the only thing that stands between yourself and your God. Then *be* the Law! *Be* the Love! *Be* the Joy of the Arisen Masters and feel Our assistance pouring forth to you at each moment each day, carrying you over many a rough place where We ourselves have already trod, for We know full well all that you must face.

Rejoice! My blessed ones, O rejoice, for these are great tidings and you may tell them to all the world, for there is born this day in the heart of each man the Christ child, the unfolding Flame of Love, and as he nurtures and cares for that Flame it will smolder and burst into a mighty conflagration of eternal perfection.

This is the joyous news. Each one has his opportunity and that opportunity is eternal. Then why delay? Accept your responsibility! Accept your God dominion, and go forward together as loving children before the Great Dawn of Life. Give of yourself, for I tell you that when you give of yourself you give of Me, and everyone of My Brothers. You cannot give truly until you have given of yourself.

Know always that however much you may desire to help another, assistance to the other can most perfectly be given by rendering first your call to that Great and Mighty I AM Presence within you, then pouring forth your love, your understanding, your peace, and qualify those outpourings with the perfection that can alone come from the Arisen Host and from your own God self. Let it sweep forth infolding the beloved one you wish to assist and that one will receive a charge of Light and beauty and perfection untouched and uncontaminated by human feeling.

Let your attention be ever upon the Most High, the Living God within you. Do not permit the affairs of the outer world to take your attention too far afield from the perfection that is within you. Strive always to pour forth love to your own Mighty God self in gratitude and thanksgiving for life and all that life holds for you. When you have done that, let that love flow out to all the world. Be a great Beacon of Light that pours forth love at every moment. Be not afraid to pour forth love. You will make no mistake if you do. Let that love flowing from your heart, from the cosmic heart of you, be as a great river that sweeps aside all obstacles, infolds all resisting things, and goes on ever expanding until it meets with itself again to become a great wave infolding you and raising you into your perfection, your permanent, your eternal freedom.

Though you remain here in the atmosphere of earth giving your service and helping mankind, remember that as long as you remain in the physical octave your service will be limited to those things that are physical, at least to a large degree. But once you have conquered and overcome those things which We know as death and fear, hate and anger, doubt and suspicion, once you have overcome those things of lower human vibratory action, you will rise up like the wings of morning and you will be free to serve in even greater capacity.

Service, dear ones, is love, for love is the essence of all life and it is life. Take time to love. O how beautiful, how glorious this world will be when humanity has learned to pour forth love and blessings to each other, to things and conditions. What a dreadful state it is in now when its own doubts and fears deprive it of the greatest joy that can possibly come to it, and yet, deep within man's heart he longs, O how he longs and cries out in the stillness of his self-created night, for that love which he needs so earnestly.

O My beloved children, tonight as I stand here with you I infold you in the mantle of My Peace. Know always that you are here in the Father's House, that you are one with God, the I AM that I AM. Accept that in its fullness, that any remaining doubts and fears may be swept aside and transmuted in the brilliant blazing Fire of Forgiveness.

This is the season of the year when mankind thinks so frequently of Me. Their attention turns to Me, sometimes questioning, sometimes with longing, so frequently with pathetic misunderstanding. But at least the attention does turn to Me and I am enabled by the use of these rays of attention coming from a multitude of mankind to pour back to humanity thoughts, feelings, and energies of Myself, which serve as anchoring points for greater Light that can be released into the consciousness of mankind who think of Me.

Lift up your heads, O blessed students. Stand firm in your knowledge of the one God that beats your hearts. Accept the greatness of Light and the Oneness of Light. Be the fulfillment of Love. O practice this! Put the activity of mind aside for a while, if only for a brief while, and be a being of Love that knows naught else but Love. Be that! O I tell you with all the earnestness of My heart that if you will but experience for a brief moment the ecstasy, the supreme eternal Joy of giving Love, first to life and then to all that shares life with you, your happiness will infold you so bountifully and so perfectly that you will know what We have called the Kingdom of Heaven and you will live there with the Angels.

XII

A NEW CYCLE

by Saint Germain and Urlando

You must realize that in this unusual service which We are attempting to render the power of your attention is very great and as your attention is turned to the Realms of Light in a most natural and normal way We can release tremendous forces of energy into your worlds to do your bidding and thus your every conscious command will be intensified tremendously. It is very difficult sometimes for the outer human consciousness to realize that there is nothing unusual or different about an activity which it cannot see or hear, and thus it is that many times you will pass all unknowingly by the great opportunity that stands there before you, for what individuals do not see they are not conscious of. O what a blessing it will be when mankind comes to realize the reality of the Inner realms of Light and Love, of the Great Realms of Beauty and Perfection, and thus they will be able to tune into those same forces which I just mentioned to receive the benefit of them and thus become master of their worlds through the activity of Love.

O dear ones, if you will only hold in your consciousness the reality of the ascension and the great victory which you are winning, the great sea of Light and Perfection which is yours! It is not only that you have gathered together to be perfect masters, but as you know, this Focus of Light is dedicated to the maintaining of the Light and the Truth upon this planet. It is quite imperative that a group of people be raised up strong enough and harmonious enough who can work together during this period of change, for I tell you this period of change which we have entered into is the most terrific change that has ever come to this planet.

The world has entered into a new cycle, a cycle which will bring great physical destruction upon the Earth. I do not tell you this to alarm you or to cause your attention to turn to that destruction, I tell you this because you must see that through all this destruction there is a great blessing coming forth. Perfection must triumph! How beautiful will be that day when a majority of mankind understand that and, dear ones, humanity will, a majority of mankind will understand that. The day will come when a majority of the people upon this planet will understand this Law, and when that day arrives discord and destruction will cease! Mark My word! That is why you will see vast numbers of mankind being removed from this planet. This will continue until the students of Light and those who seek the constructive way of life are predominant.

The very doctrine of Peace which you have had for hundreds of years has been taken up by those who seek to destroy, and used as a disarming implement and an implement to rule the senses, to cause a shirking of responsibility, a lessening of the desire for good, until mankind has accepted the lethargy that comes with the feeling that peace is sleep and rest. No more serious misconception could ever have been given, for I tell you dear ones, that peace is the greatest activity in the world!

How We long to take away from mankind its petty, selfish, narrow viewpoints! When We look upon the Earth and see blessed, blessed humanity struggling about, wallowing as it were in the filth of its own creation, how We long to reach down and just raise them up into Our octave, and yet We cannot, because do you see if We did that humanity would never learn, and thus, unless humanity learns, what is the purpose of it?

The Great Law of Life, the Great Law of Justice and Balance that governs immutably throughout the Earth has decreed that each individual must take his own responsibility. Every individual must stand squarely on his own feet and face the Great Blazing, Dazzling Light of his own Presence, conquering all.

I tell you in no uncertain terms, you must learn to pour forth love and blessings no matter what the appearance may be. If someone does something which you do not like, pour forth love and blessings. If you see destruction and discord on every hand, train yourself to look at it unflinchingly and pour forth love and blessings. *Pour it forth!* Do not just intellectually think love, for love is not thought, it is feeling, and you must pour it forth as a mighty living thing, cleansing, raising and purifying.

I want you to get the feeling of that—get the feeling of your obligation to man, to life, that will cause you to stand firm and true in the great task which lies ahead. Never feel that you are working too hard. Never accept that you are tired or weary. Refuse those human things. I do not mean now that you should become unbalanced in any way. You must have sufficient sleep, and when you go to bed and your thoughts and feelings are all disturbed because of some one or some thing and you cannot sleep, be sure you call on the Law of Forgiveness and then, even though it may seem most painful to you, call off the names of those who have been disturbing you during the day and pour forth love and blessings to them, and you will quickly fall asleep and be in the arms of your Presence.

Every one of you is being used at the Inner levels during the period when your body is at rest. A tremendous service is being performed in that fashion. Some of you from time to time bring back portions of the memory of it, but I suggest in all love that you do not discuss that with others because when you do that We find it necessary to draw the veil more closely about your eyes that you do not bring back any of it until you can move forth consciously from the outer to the Inner, never having to have the veil drawn against you. These mighty Inner realms of Light and Love are real, blessed ones. The Truth of Life has at last been given!

O dear ones, be so happy, be so joyous, be so free. Feel free to be yourself. Feel free to call the Presence into action, and dear ones, do not let anyone be a drain upon you. Stand by yourself. Give all the assistance that is necessary but never feel a sense of irritation. Whenever you feel some such human action begin instantly to call on the Fire of Forgiveness, take your attention off the appearance, and call the Presence into action to release such Light as to dissolve any such appearance. I tell you, dear ones, so many times a little appearance, a little suggestion will find its way into your world and because you do not turn on it quickly enough and get it out while it is still just a little thing, it grows, because your energy feeds it, and pretty soon you have a real battle on your hands. How much more simple and joyous it is to turn on it instantly and throw it right out. That way you will keep your world clear and there will be no great battle to handle because you never permitted a small battle to take place. Just throw out the things you do not wish to take place and remember, if you do not feed them they cannot get in, if you will make your application.

It is amazing how readily the individual will accept My words provided what I say fits into his desire world, but the minute I give a law which means that he will have to make some application and really go to work to handle himself, how quick the human is to rebel. Well, it makes no difference to Me who rebels or who does not. This Law shall go forth and humanity shall have the blessing of this great Truth! Humanity needs it and shall have it!

Please feel and accept My Love and Blessing charging your worlds with Light, with Freedom and Truth. Know that your I AM Presence, the Great God Power of you, is the Commanding Presence, the absolute ruler of your own activity, of your world. Feel the assurance in your Presence, that in your presence you can do no wrong and all things with God are perfect, and that if you enter into the I AM you have entered into the Perfection of God. Accept the authority that comes with that Perfection.

True love, Divine Love, is a giving, the surrendering of all things to God. Human love is a demanding, a curiosity, a desiring, a possessing, a craving, and is not to be compared with the awe inspiring essence of life which is the pure Love of God which fills your every atom. Pour forth that love divinely, and watch your feeling worlds, and know that We who have guided you for ages are still guiding you and that you have nothing to fear.

Look always forward and know that to the one who looks forward advancement is certain. To the one who looks backward disappointment will always overwhelm. There is only one action of Light and that is ever expanding, ever increasing Perfection. Accept that for your own heart and know that the Light of God never fails, and We who in a measure represent that Light of God for the humanity of Earth have not and will not fail, regardless of the weakness of human vehicles. We stand supreme and shall render our service to mankind whether or not they accept such service. The Truth will prevail and the Light shall radiate and shall awaken all men within their hearts. The joy and happiness of love shall burn ever brighter and the I AM Presence, the Eternal Christ within each heart, shall be the ruling Presence, the Great King of all creation!

Blessed children of the Light, accept, O accept what is being done for you. Your own Presence and the radiation from the Arisen Masters and from the Great White Brotherhood will never fail you. Stand firm and true to that which you know. Harmonize yourself and pour forth love to one another. Listen to the great motto: *To Know, to Dare, to Do, and to be Silent.* Let it speak in your hearts. Mold your actions accordingly, and know that no harm can befall you, for you are My children, you have become My family, and you will see that the Light, when understood, without fanaticism and without pressure, always protects its own.

*   *   *

It has not been My intention to release this magnificent information to the children of Earth that they might profit selfishly. This information has been released to them that they may improve themselves and assist others in raising their consciousness into the pathway of Light, where Freedom, Beauty, and Perfection awaits each and every one.

If sometimes you find it a little difficult to make your

application, will you not remember this: If there is something in your feelings which makes you doubt that you will
have the answer to your call, that doubt is going to have to be
removed before the full power of your Presence can flow
forth. Therefore, do you not see if you doubt My reality or
that of your Presence, or Its power to work through you, then
even your calls will have to wait, in a measure, until those
doubts can be dissolved and removed; but know you can call
to the Presence to remove those doubts, and when that
sincere desire is present it is a very simple matter to clear out
anything that might remain and very quickly have the actual
proof of the reality of these Great Laws and practical proof of
that which has come forth.

In order that you may definitely have the fulfillment of
your calls, will you not believe while you are making the calls
at least? Do you not see that if you make a call to your
Presence on the one hand and on the other have a recurring
feeling of doubt that the call probably will not be answered
anyway, don't you see you merely interfere with the full
power of the Presence flowing forth which could so quickly
answer the call? While you are calling, silence your doubt and
give all faith and confidence to your Presence that Its full
power may flow forth unmolested to fulfill your every
command. As you begin to gain a momentum in silencing the
feeling you will quickly rise above the outer world. Turn your
attention to that Great Presence and know the Mighty Life
and Light which is Its Heart!

URLANDO speaks:

You can so charge your world with Light and Love that
everywhere you move there will be an aura about you, a
fragrance which would be noticeable in the physical octave.
You might think that it would be a little bit embarrassing, but
it wouldn't be. I assure you that it is far better to give off a
fragrance of Divine Love than some of the fragrance that
some of mankind like to give off! Man, unfortunately, has
gotten itself into the way of thinking that any odor that
comes from it is unpleasant and the only pleasant odor they

could have would be artificial. That is exactly wrong. In truth it is just the other way about, for the natural expression, the natural fragrance of the individual is one of great beauty, and it is only the human consciousness which creates the opposite impression. Will that not be a marvelous day, blessed ones, when we may have perfectly natural things in the physical octave, and I tell you that that day is not far off.

Before very long, as I believe you have been told previously, there will be means of transportation released to you, the children of Earth, that will certainly indicate to you the great strides, the great progress being made in the raising of the consciousness of mankind. There are a number of inventions at the present time already released into the physical world, waiting to be released to the general public, which more than double the fastest speed known to man so far, and that is not the limit. Humanity has just begun to scratch the surface of speed.

You must realize that the time may come when travel between the planets at the outer levels will be just as practical as it is today from the inner levels, and when that time comes you must understand that man will have to go a great deal more rapidly than they do now, otherwise they would have several appearances to contend with.

When you enter into the activity of the I AM Presence and realize that It is the Oneness of all things, and that Oneness is everywhere present at one and the same instant, you will begin to comprehend in which world you are manifesting and understand how your calls are answered instantly, and begin to build a momentum which will bring the manifestation of your calls. However, I would like to make this one suggestion: In calling to your Presence to release any particular thing to you be absolutely certain that you call for something that will be of benefit to more than just yourself.

If you wish to be happy; if you wish to be free; if you wish to have the fullness of God's Love and Light flowing through you, never, never, never misuse God's Law by demanding things for yourself selfishly. If you make a command to the Presence for something that you wish, you have every right and authority, as long as it is not for your selfish use. I cannot prompt you too earnestly about that—to avoid the desire to accumulate or have power, position, wealth, or any other thing for the sake of the thing itself. All of those things can be used provided you remain master of them and they are dispensed through your own beneficence. But I plead with you, do not ever form the idea that you have come so close to God that you as a physical being control Gods opulence, for just as soon as you do you are in for a terrific fall! Just observe the outpicturing about you. Be wise and profit by the experience of others.

Remember, when you ask the Presence for something it will come forth! Be sure, therefore, that you ask for others, for as you ask for others and begin to acquire the confidence which you should have, you will have the power to call forth whatever you require. Then with these great powers in your grasp, do you not see how imperative it is to discipline yourself so that you do not command something which would be selfish or that would injure others? The full Power of the Universe is at your finger tips! It awaits your call. It awaits your disciplined call, but through the activity of your Presence. The full power will never be released until you have learned to discipline yourself.

Saint Germain continues:

Accept the full power of life as it flows through you, flooding your world with the fullness of all things. Know that your Presence is at the same level as the Presence of the Great Ones, and in that you stand at one with the Arisen Masters' Consciousness. Feel the full power of that Life, that you may go forth quickly raising the consciousness of mankind everywhere, raising all into the beauty and perfection of the New Golden Age.

XIII

THE INNER REALMS

by Saint Germain and Cyclopea

Thousands of mankind are ready to turn to this Light. Not to any one individual, not to a group of individuals, but those who can teach them the Law of Life. Make no mistake about it, you have learned the Law of Life, there is no other. Unless one understands his own God Presence and will call to that Presence and accept the help of the Arisen Masters who have gone before and proved the way of Life, then he does not understand the Law of Life.

When you find others who are in need of assistance, please do not step in and tell them what they should do. Call to the I AM Presence to render the assistance that is necessary; turn your attention to the God Presence, and do not attempt to solve it humanly. When you find an individual who requires assistance say to that one: "Dear friend, I will help you. Feel that I am your friend and that I am standing by to give every assistance, but knowing the Law, I feel that it would be wise for you to turn to your Presence of Life, God, which made us, and then divine assistance can come forth. May I show you how to make the call that will set you free?" If you will only do that you will save yourself and your friend, or the one whom you are assisting, from such great suffering and wasted energy. Do not say to that one: "Well, it is your problem, you call to your Presence." That is not kind and that is not the Law. It is true the other person has a Presence and it is true he must make the call to release the energy for the outpicturing of what is required, but if you will only charge yourselves with kindness you can be such radiant channels in assisting to bring that forth. Do you not see that each one is your brother? Then why be superior to that one? But rather, through your conscious stand, your own Power of Light, seek to raise his consciousness.

Another thing which I feel it would be wise for Me to give you a little reminder upon is the activity of turning your attention to the Inner realms. Never forget that at the Inner realms all things are possible, all things good, all things bad. Yes, dear ones, the Inner realms are far more vast than the outer, and sinks lower and rises higher. Therefore, just because you have learned to turn your attention to the Inner realms does not mean that you have made contact with the Arisen Masters' Law of Life or the radiation of the presence of a Master.

There are gradations of progress at the Inner levels far more vast and far more numerous than you will find in the outer world, but you have the key whereby you may determine what is acting. You have the knowledge which, when used, will stand as a living bulwark of protection, regardless of where you move, in the Inner or outer world. Accept your Presence in the Living Flame of Life from out the Central Sun. Accept your Oneness with that Sun of Life, and pour forth your energy at all times. Know there is no power can say you nay when you ask the Presence to bring Divine Order and Divine Love wherever you move.

When you turn your attention to the Inner and find yourself disturbed by unpleasant dreams, negative, vicious thoughts and feelings, even suggestions sometimes of greed and lust, blessed ones, just because that seems to come from the Inner does not mean that it is a reality. There is only one reality and that is the Living Presence of God within you. If what you receive from the Inner or outer does not mean perfection, dismiss it and avoid it as you would a serpent. Call to your Presence to stand guard over you and when you find yourself about to experience an inner activity which is less than the perfection which you know should exist, for goodness sakes get out of it—move into the activity of your Higher Mental Body or your Presence, or get back into your own physical body. Do not permit those things to dwell in your consciousness and do not discuss them!

It is possible for each and every one under this radiation now to have many magnificent Inner experiences at night and bring back consciously what has been given. If you talk about it, it will not take place. If you wish to make progress you must stand alone. You must go by yourself, face your own God Presence serenely and say: *"Let Thy will, not mine be done. Make of me, O I AM Presence, that which I AM, that which I was in the beginning. I accept now the full Christ Light enfolding me. I give no power to human creation, and ever abide in the Great Glorious Heart of Love to render my assistance, my service to mankind everywhere."*

O, it is not an easy pathway which you have chosen, but it is the only pathway which leads to your own complete victory in the ascension. There has been so much doubt and fear cast upon the activity of the ascension that there are many who doubt its reality and feel something amiss. You are now receiving the absolutely correct information concerning the Ascension, which is the same identical information given several years ago, and that is correct! The ascension is possible for every individual, and I think I ought to know what I am talking about! It is the goal for mankind, but My precious ones, that goal cannot be attained through any conceivable short cut, for until you have rendered a service to your brothers you have not earned the right.

CYCLOPEA speaks:

Many times I have observed the sincere student will not release the full power of which he is capable in making a call for a simple thing. It is wise while learning to have a sense of balance such as that, but all too many times the individual refuses to release sufficient energy for the thing required rather than too much. You will know that you have released too much energy if in the release of energy you upset the feelings of others or you begin to have pour in upon you that for which you have called in far greater abundance than you can use. If your call is for money sufficient to do what is required and you suddenly find yourself deluged with vast quantities of money, you will know that you have released too much energy in that direction.

I wish you to understand that it does not take vast mental powers to be a good student of Light. Sincerity is much more important than a vast intellect. Humility is of far greater value than experience or education. Divine Love is the greatest assistance of all.

Know that there is no hiding thoughts, motives, subtle human desires, all of those things which you do not wish to have anyway and can never be hidden from your own God self, the Mighty I AM. What a great sense of joy and happiness, of freedom, comes to the individual when he realizes that he does not have to hide anything, because he cannot do so anyway. Then he knows that truth, honesty, openness are the only qualities, and knowing that, the Light blazes forth in all its glory.

Saint Germain continues:

Mankind must have its attention turned to these Mighty Laws of Life. The consciousness of humanity has been such as to ridicule many of the sacred teachings of life. I wish you to understand this: When I say certain ones ridicule the teachings of Life I do not in any way mean they are vicious or destructive—they are merely children who do not understand. Humanity always has and always will ridicule things they do not understand. It is an element of human consciousness that refuses to accept anyone more intelligent than they are.

If you are going forward into the Arisen state rendering a service to mankind you have to be dependable at every step. You must remember that your minds are to be strong, your hearts strong and brave, your feelings in perfect order—which means you are going to have to listen with a calm feeling even to the most destructive statements, even against the Light. I do not mean that you have to condone discord of others, certainly not, for that is to move into the activity of it. You must, if you wish your freedom, if you wish your progress, *positively stand alone!* I wish you to understand that. It makes no difference what the tie may seem to be from the outer standpoint. You as an individualized focus of life came forth from the heart of God by yourself and into that you will return by yourself. You can take no one with you. You are yourself an individualized focus of God, the I AM Presence, and as such you are never more nor less than that.

It does not make any difference how near or dear some one may be to you. It does not make any difference what the connection may be, either inwardly, spiritually or physically, the truth remains that you as an individual go forward according to your own application. And may I suggest you stop trying to lean on one another. Call to your I AM Presence, your ever present help, turn to It to surge through you in a never ending stream of love and blessings. Do not take into your world infirmities, negative suggestions of others. Stand calm and serene if you stand in the midst of turmoil, but refuse acceptance into your world of any of that turmoil.

You stand on the threshold of life and before you stretches the glory of the ages. About you stand those of the human race who need your assistance, your guidance. You do not have to waste time ever, blessed ones. May I urge you to stop feeling ever that the long, long day is still ahead and then comes the long, long night. Call to your Presence to transmute that feeling. If there is something in your world that tells you that you are wasting your time, that is the Voice of the Presence that commands you to get busy. There is no limit to what you can do when you accept the reality of the Great God Presence and accept the Presence within, that living Source of Life.

Remember to give instantaneous obedience without even asking why a command is being given, because I tell you dear ones, if that ever occurs and you are not ready, you alone will be the one who will pay the penalty.

Mankind for centuries has drawn upon itself its own doom. Civilizations have risen and civilizations have fallen since the beginning of time upon this planet and every single rise has come about because of the quickening in the vibratory action of the cells that composed the structure of individuals in embodiment at that time, and every falling away has come about because the vibratory action has lowered, for the individual has ceased to turn attention to progress and has turned aside to satisfy himself.

The I AM Presence is your treasure house of all good and perfect things and as you turn your attention to It you obey the Great Law of the One in the most perfect, simple and beautiful way. When you turn your attention to your Presence you are one with your source, for where your attention is there you are.

In turning your attention to your I AM Presence and holding your attention not only there but upon the perfect thing which you wish done, you are able to go forward to whatever other tasks may be a part of your activity and still your attention and your desire for the perfect thing will be assisted by every act that you do. For instance, let us take an example: Suppose you need ten thousand dollars—which is as easy to call forth as ten cents, I assure you, providing you release the energy. Naturally you will have to release more energy for ten thousand dollars than you will for ten cents, but just exactly the same law is acting. The trouble with most of mankind is that they are too lazy to release enough energy for ten thousand dollars and so they don't get it, they get ten cents.

Now we are considering that you require ten thousand dollars. All right, you turn your attention to your Presence and you call that your attention be maintained there, that your desires always be for the perfect thing. Now, holding your attention there you are still able to turn your attention to something else. That may seem like a contradiction but it is not. The I AM Presence knows all things. Call first with your attention upon the Presence, then with your attention upon the perfect thing that you require, in this case ten thousand dollars. Just make the call that the Presence release the ten thousand dollars to you, see it and possess it in your hands and use, and then go forward with whatever you are doing, washing dishes, going to work, performing your regular daily services, but keep your attention and keep calling to your Presence that the attention will be fixed upon what you desire, and I tell you the way will open for each and every one of you to be supplied with ten thousand dollars just as soon as you do it that way.

The difficulty with humanity has been—and here is the difficulty which so many of the blessed students have had—in that they have called for the ten thousand dollars and called and called, and the only energy they have released in that direction was the actual energy of the calls; therefore, they have accepted the asking, beseeching consciousness and it has become: "O I AM Presence give me."

Now the Law is, you must give before you can receive. Therefore, if you require ten thousand dollars you must be prepared to give ten thousand dollars worth of energy to get it, for I tell you, you cannot get it or anything until you release the necessary energy. Therefore, when you require ten thousand dollars make up your mind you will release the ten thousand dollars worth of energy for it. The Presence has an unlimited amount of energy for your use; It has an unlimited amount of money for your use, but you are the one who must release the energy. I think if you will read this over and study it and call to have the full understanding released to you, you will have wonderful results.

Many times I have heard students say: "If I only had so much money," and the consciousness is upon what could be done "if," but that "if" grows and grows and grows and presently the individual has just accepted in his feelings and his consciousness that he never will be able to get more than a certain stipulated amount, for which he has already built up a consciousness.

Learn to accept that with the Presence all things are possible, then with that acceptance turn your attention to your Presence, taking the consciousness of having that which is required and take the responsibility for releasing sufficient energy to get it. Why dear ones, you know mankind is lazy! I would say to you that 999 people out of 1,000 are too lazy ever to have as much money as they need! It isn't because they don't have the ability; it isn't because they don't need the money; it is just because they will not exert themselves past a certain point. I have observed it in almost 100% of the cases. An individual will be very enthusiastic about his job, his work, which is the channel temporarily for his supply, and he will go to work until he gets his first pay check. Then he says: "I have earned this, now I shall enjoy myself," and away goes the energy and the money, and then comes the next week and the same activity and the same result, and the next and the next.

Now the students of Light shall understand that if acquiring money is the goal, you cannot go forward one day and then turn aside and say, "O well, I certainly made progress today." You will never go past a very few steps. They work five, five and a half, sometimes six days and then they say, "I certainly deserve to take a day off." Then they dissipate their forces and have to begin all over again next day. O I know, life would seem very harsh if we had all work and no play, I am not saying that. I am saying, if you would be steadfast about what you have to do there is no greater enjoyment. The greatest happiness will come to you through your I AM Presence, for everything else you contact will leave a bad taste with you. You blessed ones have advanced too far to get lasting pleasure out of anything except Light. You may just as well accept that for it is true, and to the extent that you accept that Light will you find happiness and peace.

The Laws of Life which We give you are absolutely practical in every detail. There is no short cut to perfection and there is no way by which you can profit several fold and have the Presence release things to you which you haven't earned. And may I suggest that you not be foolish and try to withdraw from your storehouse things that have been drawn there for your final victory. That has been done by old students until they find themselves practically depleted. Their Causal bodies are packed with Light and magnificent momentum, and yet if they insist on drawing that forth now rather than constantly trying to put more there, they are like the prodigal son who insisted on wasting his Father's heritage, until finally awakening as to what he has done, turns around and comes back into the Father's House.

I do not mean by this now that you should become miserly, for you know the Law, that you should give and give that you yourself may be free, but I wish you to understand that the only things you can give are the things that you have earned now, rather than counting on the earnings of previous embodiments.

The time of walking around in a daze must cease if you wish to make permanent progress. The laziness and lethargy of humanity is appalling! Some one will find out there is a duty which he has to perform, which may be sweeping the floor, shoveling the snow off the sidewalk, or digging a ditch, and the individual will go to do that and just not move a muscle more than necessary, getting through with it in such a slow, painful way. Now what good is that? They haven't released any energy, they have been complaining to themselves of the injustice of life, and what are they worth when it is done?

Dear ones, if a floor has to be swept, grab the broom and sweep it, and rejoice you are the channel for doing it! It is appalling how mankind insists on feeling sorry for themselves because they have things to do. There are thousands of people who spend their time just sitting, wondering if they are ever going to have to move very rapidly and hoping that they won't. Isn't that appalling? But I tell you that is the condition of mankind today, for they have fallen into this lethargic state. They accept such great limitation and they won't bestir themselves to get out of it.

I would suggest that you learn to walk with your head held high, your shoulders back, and walk as if you were going some place—and I don't mean a funeral! Walk with purpose, with light in your eye, and a light step! I know you will attract attention to yourself when you first do this and your human will rebel at you, but you get your human down on the floor and step on it! I don't wish to suggest now that you do anything ridiculous. Don't start running. Be sane and balanced about this, but for goodness sakes, let us begin to take that pride in being a student of Light which is essential if you wish others to take a pride in it also.

I also suggest in your work in your various homes, that you do it absolutely perfectly or don't do it at all. The Arisen Master is the one Who has learned to do every task perfectly. Never leave things half completed. If you are starting out to accomplish something, it doesn't make any difference what interrupts, see that it is done. There are exceptions, but if something does interrupt you, go back and finish it and see you don't have to ask anybody to do it for you, and rejoice in the privilege.

To answer your question regarding thought and attention, I think I can clear that point up for you best by going back to what I mentioned a short while ago. Where your attention is there you are. Now your thought is the pattern that the attention forms. Your conscious thought is the thought and the attention which is woven together by desire. When you wish to call to your I AM Presence, then turn your attention to the requirement—say the ten thousand dollars which I mentioned—then go forward doing something else. The human likes to stick up its head and say, "Well, how in the world can I have my attention upon the Presence, upon ten thousand dollars, and upon sweeping the floor, or something?" Well, dear ones, the simple truth is that when you turn your attention to the Presence you must recognize the I AM Presence is in all things. Then in recognizing that you recognize that the Presence is also in the requirement— the ten thousand dollars which we are still using as an example. Then you also recognize the Presence is acting in your sweeping of the floor. Thus you will see that your attention is upon the I AM Presence. Your thought, which is the activity of your attention, is the pattern, for the attention is probably upon the sweeping of the floor, or should be. The conscious thought, the desire, is held upon the ten thousand dollars and has nothing to do with sweeping the floor, yet they are all one. Or, you are engaged in things in the outer world, and yet all that time your attention may be upon the I AM Presence. You see, dear ones, you are unlimited.

You will recall in *Unveiled Mysteries* the explanation was given as to consciousness, projected consciousness, and how it is possible for the individual to be conscious of one tree and a whole forest. Thus it is with every child of God, every individualized Flame of Life. That is why you will find it absolutely possible and practical, the most joyous activity of your life, to accept the Presence acting in everything and then keep using the activity and be happy in rendering some outer service, while at the same time you can qualify what you are doing in the outer world with perfection. Think of those points and you will see the Great Law acting there.

You see, dear ones, it is the expansion of the same activity which permits Me to be present with you here at this moment and at this same identical moment to be conducting an activity in Arabia, and if I wished to be I could be a lot of others places too. Now each one of you has that same quality and are not limited in any way. Naturally you will have your greatest progress when you combine all of those activities, but the imperative thing is to turn to the Presence first, and when you call to the Presence and turn your attention there first, seeing the Presence in everything you do, then you do all things together and all things become one in your world.

You will always observe that the individual who is doing the thing that he likes to do is happy, and why is that? Because he is at-one with himself. Let us suppose there is some one who has invented a new type of steamboat. The idea for that steamboat may have come forth while he was doing some other kind of work entirely and it seemed he would be very unhappy until he could get to the place where he would work on the steamboat. Yet when that time did arrive he would work consciously, physically upon the one thing and he would have become one with his desire, so he would be happy. But if the individual knew the law he could arrive at the happy state so much more rapidly, instantly, if he could turn and recognize the I AM Presence and recognize the task which he might be doing at the moment, and thus it would be all one. Then recognizing the Presence he would be able to move forward with the speed of Light and bring about the fulfillment of the activity, and what would have taken years would take only weeks.

I cannot mention enough the imperative need of turning always to the Presence and becoming used to the fact that the I AM Presence is within you at all times and that you have every right and every authority to turn to It at all times.

XIV

THE DAWN OF THE GOLDEN CENTURY

by Saint Germain

I assure you that every call that you make, every earnest, sincere call you send forth to your I AM Presence and any of the Arisen Host of Light is answered instantly. You do not have to wait for the fulfillment of your every conscious command. The activity of human consciousness has for many centuries been such as to make the individual often doubt his ability to receive assistance from the Presence, yet the Presence does not doubt, every call is answered. Every time you put your conscious faith and acceptance upon that, instantly doubt will stop acting in your world. I wish you to understand, however, that you should never apply to the extent that you become off balance. This is mighty important to remember.

As you gain a momentum in decreeing for any particular thing, say five dollars, you make your dynamic call for that to come into your hands and use. Presently the five dollars comes forth and then, because the student sees clearly one way in which this is to come forth, he goes on decreeing on the same problem, asking for another five dollars, and another, etc., until the time arrives when he will have to stop that in order to have the release of it. You can only gather your momentum to a certain place, according to the progress you have made. At that point it is necessary that you let go of it.

Never hesitate to release all the energy and all the power of which you are capable in controlling your own human. Silence it even if you have to shout at it a little, but be very careful that you do not shout at any other human. That is the thing that creeps in so many times. Recognize your own God dominion and absolute authority that is in the I AM Presence, but do not feel that that authority extends over the human of other individuals. It does not! Let us understand that! The authority of the Presence does extend over all human individuals and from that Cosmic authority all authority comes, but you as one individual only have authority over yourself as an individual. The I AM Presence is the individualization of all individualizations. Read this over carefully when you have it written and study it and you will see it will mean a great deal to you.

I should like to mention something to you concerning the activity of patience, for it is a quality that many of you will have to use in the future. I do not mean now that you should have patience to the point of lying down on the job and saying: "the Presence will take care of it." You must release your energy, accept that it is going to take place now, and anticipate it with all the joy and happiness of your being, but when it does not occur just at the moment you think it should and you say, "well now look, it hasn't happened," that is looking for manifestations rather than to your Presence for the opportunity of serving.

Always be patient with one another. Take time to be kind. So many times just when something beautiful happens one will be so thrilled and happy and excited he will just leap forward into action, and in the leaping forward, just a little off balance, he may cause a little unhappiness or discomfiture for some brother or sister. Take time to be kind. Be thoughtful and considerate. Call to your Presence to charge you always with Arisen Master discrimination, peace, balance, energy, life, and happiness. Feel that sustaining Presence entering into every act during the day. If you accomplish any one thing, after you accomplish it turn your attention to your Presence and accept the sustaining power of your Presence pouring into your accomplishment as it is made. Thus you will very quickly qualify your world with permanency. For everything which you do consciously, which is a real and constructive accomplishment, give praise and thanks to the Light of God within you and then feel the permanency of the victory of the Presence.

Never tire of calling to your Presence. Never tire of seeking to live the Arisen Masters' way of life. Always that perfection is possible for you. Let your hearts sing in love and gratitude day after day.

This activity which has been drawn forth here, although it seems similar to you in many respects to the former activity, may I again remind you that it is nothing like the other at all. I wish you to understand that and have it firmly in your consciousness, for this New Dispensation does not have certain qualities in it which the other did, just as the other did not have some of the qualities which you now have. Even despite the similarity in phraseology and in the method of conducting meetings and in the method of My coming, dear ones, remember that this is altogether different. It is new, more perfect, more lasting than anything that has come forth to this date.

I wish you to be very well informed and in close touch with all that goes on. Each one of you should listen to at least one news broadcast a day, and keep yourselves informed of what goes on in the papers too, but do not take those things into your consciousness. You are learning to be master now. Learn to look upon a condition and keep it from your world. Call your Presence into action to assist in this. That is mastery, for that is exactly what I have to do every day. As any one of the Arisen Masters come near enough to mankind to work with them, He couldn't be a Master if He refused to work with humanity or accepted its conditions into His world. You must do the same. Be able to look upon a situation but refuse to accept it in your own world.

Feel the Love Flame of the Pure Christ within your heart at all times, even when you go into a very humble situation among humble surroundings, speaking with humble people—feel that Flame of the Pure Christ within you, and let that Flame of Love flow forth from you. Feel it pouring forth from every cell of your being, from your finger tips, from your hands, from your heart area, your entire head and throat. Feel it pour forth and see it expand to enfold all of mankind everywhere. Know that when you as an individual see that activity you are God, the I AM Presence seeing Its Perfection, and thus Perfection will come into your world and you will assist in inspiring Perfection in the world of those with whom you come in contact.

It is not possible for an individual—the individualized Flame of God—to go forth into his or her eternal victory until the enemies of doubt or fear have been removed from his consciousness and his world. If you wish your victory and freedom you will have to make your application to weed out doubt and fear. It makes no difference whether you wish to have harmony in your world or not, I come to give you the way to your freedom, happiness, and victory. It is up to you what you shall do, and your doubt and fear can rob you of it. It is up to you entirely.

When you know positively the reality of this Great Law, why will you permit activities of a negative nature to take your attention? Do you not see in this matter of attention lies the whole of the Law, of the Truth? Your attention and your feeling at inner levels becomes one, and thus as you master one of the great God attributes you will have learned mastery of another and another, and you will be master of your world. It is not possible for you to go forward into Victory and Freedom, which you have a right to expect, unless you learn to govern these things.

You must remember that this is the coming together of the Inner and the outer, for this is the dawn of the Golden Century, the Golden Age of Love and Peace at all times. The keynote will be Love, Love and Loyalty, Peace and Perfection, but mostly Love. Naturally you will quickly see that this change from the activities of the present day-to-day activities to the keynote of Love will be a very great change, yet it is out of this mighty crucible, this mighty seething cauldron of flame that will come the purest Love of all. Mark what I tell you, for these are mighty laws that are beginning to be expressed on the face of this Earth!

You may not completely understand or comprehend fully the import of all I give you, but in the days ahead you will see the great, unerring wisdom with which America has been guided and still is directed. It is true that there are many things wrong with every human individual. May I give you this Law which you must follow:

When you discover that an individual is permitting his human to act, and this goes especially for those who are in public office or holding responsible positions, when you observe a human quality is beginning to act in their world, as you value your progress and the safety of your world, turn your attention to your Presence and call that that individual will have God qualities take dominion there.

There has been so much criticism and condemnation, so little tolerance of the mistakes and failings of the human, because of the great determination of many to be so dynamic that they would destroy all opposition, that a great deal of harm has been done, and it is up to you in a large measure to rectify that by the power of Love and Light of the Arisen Host. That is no easy task, but every one of you has in his or her heart the complete Victory of this Light, and it is up to you what you wish to do about it! You are uniting with your fellow Americans in protecting this country. Can you not unite in protecting the Light?

So many times your attention will go to some little thing which will drive in, instead of turning to the Presence. The appearance will intensify, the discord will grow, and then the human will start in to discover who caused the discord. It doesn't make any difference who caused it. Nobody did! It is a substance that permeates the atmosphere of the Earth. It has existed for centuries and still exists in great quantity. Your obligation is not to create any more of it but call for your protection from it; to blaze more Light that the discord will disappear.

Set aside human things, set them aside and forget them. Have faith, have trust and confidence in that God Presence that created you. Is your intellect so vast as to think that there is not a power greater than itself? Do not let that erroneous conception come to you even for a moment. Give recognition to that Great God Presence, that Great I AM that I AM of you, which is all Power, all Love, all Wisdom. Accept its Light, its

Purity, its Mighty Radiance, and accept it as your final Victory. If you have that you do not need the human things any longer.

Will you now turn your attention to your Presence and to Me. Will you shut out all that the outer world keeps suggesting to you—the last conversation that you heard, the last mental picture that flashed across your mind, the last sound that penetrated your ear. Shut it out and turn your attention to your Presence, that Living White Fire of God which abides within each one of you and is the beating, pulsating Life itself. Give praise and thanks for Life, for that Flame which burns so brightly, and for the privilege you have in serving, in knowing these Great Laws.

It is a most marvelous thing that you dear people have had the instruction that gives you the privilege of calling to your own I AM Presence.

It cannot be stressed enough—you must release to those who look to you for assistance or for guidance a feeling of the Reality of the I AM Presence, and that feeling of the Reality of the Presence can only come when you have called to It, not because you have read of It, but because you have *proved* it in your experience. Then you are the proof of the I AM Presence and the Law. The whole work of the teacher to the student is to get the student to accept in his feelings the Power of God.

Be careful of the appearance world. It will make out that your best friend is your worst enemy, and the other way around. Give no power to it! Some, for no good reason, accept the appearance that individuals are telling them either truth or falsehood. I tell you, do not go by appearances! Call to your Presence to have the truth revealed to you and it will answer you with the truth.

Your I AM Presence is not concerned with personalities or creating impressions. It is not concerned with people's feelings. It is the absolute Law! Why not call to It then? Sometimes you see some little thing will take place and the individual will observe it and say, "O this individual has done this particular thing," and I tell you, dear ones, just about nine times out of ten it is absolutely not the case, because the appearance will lead you astray every time. I particularly ask you to watch this. I ask you to examine your own worlds and clear out quickly by using the Fire of Forgiveness and your own application, those wrong mental conclusions which are arrived at through partial information only.

It is far better, if you find something troubling you, to walk up to that thing or person and say to them, with your feelings under control, "Look here my friend, it seems to me this is the case. Tell me what you know of it," and you will be surprised how many times the appearance world has just led you around by the nose as it were. It is much better to do that than to let those appearances get into your world and take control of you. It is, of course, better not to let them get into your world at all, then they do not have a chance to act; however, the human sometimes has difficulty, or seems to have, in overcoming that. If the human can be put aside long enough so that the individual can turn his attention wholly to the Presence, there will be no difficulty in overcoming this particular type of human consciousness.

Learn to turn your attention to your Presence and keep it there undivided. By that I do not mean that when you turn your attention to your Presence that you should just fasten it there and never let it turn to anything else. No. But while your attention is on the Presence *let it be there and nowhere else!* Many times individuals will not take the trouble to still their worlds long enough to fasten their attention on the Presence. So many times the attention will turn to the Presence and then run off straining at the leash to countless other things. When you turn your attention to your Presence, forget everything else, and then the Presence has an opportunity of flooding Its Light into your world in great waves and streams that will quickly fill your world with Light, Love, Beauty, Perfection, Freedom, and Victory of every sort.

There is only one way to have the happiness, joy, and beauty that you have a right to expect, and that is by joyfully, willingly giving that happiness, freedom, and joy to everyone. If you wish to be free, be certain that you let everyone else be free, and the automatic result will be that your freedom will be a great gift to you, and you cannot avoid it. That is the Great Law of Life. The difficulty in the human consciousness is that it will not try these laws out but it will intellectually conclude that they will not work and will not make the attempt.

It is a marvelous thing that here upon this planet it is now possible for the full Light and Truth of Life to be released, that mankind may have it unmistakably and know without any doubt or fear the perfect course for him to pursue. Is it not a magnificent thing that there are a few who not only have that understanding but are willing to abide by that understanding regardless of human personalities. I tell you, dear ones, it is a most blessed and precious thing!

Your call to the I AM Presence always brings the answer. The question comes up of your human acceptance. The human is the qualifier and has the ability, through free will, of stepping down the perfect quality pouring down from the Presence, or qualifying it with perfection.

Regardless of the progress or lack of progress of an individual, all are on the pathway and, therefore, even though an individual may still use tobacco, liquor, and other things, this is not to stand in his way. Remember the necessity—you should without any predetermined idea pour forth love and blessings without ceasing. Your obligation is to love and bless life. When you fulfill that obligation life will love and bless you.

Remember, dear ones, life flows to you and asks nothing except that you use life abundantly. In doing that it is necessary to return life back into itself, which is what humanity has not understood. That is why they have gone on wasting their precious energy, dissipating that marvelous Light substance from the Presence, instead of raising it and sending it back to the source from whence it came.

Purity of mind, like purity of body, depends wholly upon God qualification. If you qualify yourself as a God being and see yourself constantly as an Arisen Master it will soon become impossible for you to harbor a wrong idea or to be unclean in anything that you do. If instead, you qualify yourself as the human, it will be a very easy thing for you to take into your world human thoughts, human feelings, and human conditions. Remember at all times that your discipline begins with yourself.

It is not up to you to discipline another, nor even to remind another that he might need a little discipline. Never criticize, never suggest, unless asked. If someone does a thing a thousand times wrong, better a thousand times that you remain silent rather than speak up to tell them what they should do. But instead of just being thought dumb, call to your Presence, for I tell you that Living Presence will instantly fulfill every call if you only will turn to It. Have no fear in doing so. Banish forever from your world the thought that there is anything strange in calling to God, and know that you are one with the Divinity. Be natural, normal, joyous, and happy in all of your activities.

Remember always to *still yourself*, then *call to your Presence*, then *go on your way rejoicing* that all is accomplished. This is the joyous three fold activity of life which will take you into every victory.

XV

A KUMARA BRINGS A WARNING

Godfre introduces Khubal Kumara

Saint Germain has given Me permission to give you a certain name that you may hold your consciousness upon it during this day, that during this evening you may have the experience of hearing this Blessed One speak. Not since the end of the second Golden Age has this Blessed One returned to this planet, and He will be with you tonight. When I give you His name I wish you to dwell upon it during the day, which will assist Him in coming tonight to speak to you. This Being is one of the Great Kumaras. He will be known to you as Mighty Khubal Kumara, and He will assist you in many ways.

KHUBAL KUMARA speaks:

Blessed Students of Light and mankind upon this planet: For many thousands of years there has been no activity on this Earth which corresponds in any way with the condition which you face at the present time, and thus, from out of the Great Silence, the Great Inner Realms of Light, I have come to you today after long absence. Once before, many long years ago, it was My privilege to speak to a gathering such as this, to warn them against creating the discords and the inharmonies which would eventually deprive them of the privilege which they had. Again tonight I speak to all mankind, through the Radiation of the Arisen Host and through channels of force and energy which radiate from this spot like spokes from a wheel. I speak to the hearts and minds of all individuals upon this planet: STOP WHERE YOU ARE AND FACE THE LIVING PRESENCE OF GOD, THE MIGHTY I AM WITHIN YOUR HEART! HUMANITY AWAKE! YOUR TIME IS FAR SHORTER THAN YOU KNOW!

The uncontrolled thoughts and feelings of mankind spewing forth and whirling about have formed great currents of destruction which now engulf this world. Only by great pain and suffering will those clouds be consumed, and mankind, who are the creators of those clouds of force must pay the full penalty.

Upon you, My blessed students, I shed My blessing and My protective radiance, for even though you have not known that you were My students, yet I have known of you for some little time.

The uncontrolled feeling, which is far more powerful than mankind realizes, has gone forth year after year creating, creating, creating greater density, greater accumulation, greater inharmony, and now the law of this planet, the law of the Universe itself compels that all debts be paid! Thus, those who have created discord and imperfection will find their creation returned to them, and there will be none who escape!

Dear ones, this is the hour for your planet. Such a short time remains for you to prepare. Why will you not be willing then to put aside some of the other things which seem so important to you, that you yourself may be prepared as an individual to go through this period of change and transition, that you will be purified, raised, and harmonized, and thus be free and gain your victory? I assure you, dear ones, I am not speaking idle words. The law of the Universe commands and compels this planet now to rise into its proper place in the scheme of creation. *War must cease, and shall cease, by the Power of Light itself, for that Light as of a thousand suns shall blaze throughout this planet,* and where there has been night there will be day, and where there has been day there will be brighter day!

You will find that there will be many among you throughout the world who, upon feeling this great release of Cosmic Light and Energy, this mighty pouring forth of Light from out the Great Central Sun, will be unable to stand the tremendous increase in vibratory action. Watch yourselves, watch your spoken words, your thoughts, your feelings, for with the tremendous increase it will be a very simple matter for an individual to once lose control in a small thing, to lose complete control, and thus all hope of permanent victory in this embodiment.

There are those who, because of the discord and imperfection which came into the life of the precious Messengers, have scoffed at the reality of these Great Laws, or at the reality of the Messengers, or these Precious Children, and I say to such scoffers and doubters: Beware! I do not threaten you, I only say: BEWARE! for your scoffing and your doubting will keep you from your own freedom and victory in the Light! Mankind has had its opportunity to accept this Light, for there are thousands upon thousands who have had it presented to them, yet today only such a small handful remain of those who really believe the great Principles of Life which Saint Germain has taught you.

Dear ones, this same condition has come upon this planet before, though never in such an intensified activity. The last four times that discord reached this point humanity was able to have a few scattered groups throughout the planet which remained in embodiment and assisted in bringing down the Great Truths and purposes of life unto the present time. Previous to those last four times there was one occasion when the discord and imperfection of this planet reached such a height that only a very few were permitted to remain in physical embodiment at all. Were it not for the calls of the students, were it not for the fact that Saint Germain has labored so ceaselessly, that Jesus, Godfre, the Great Divine Director and Others have helped so tremendously, at this time your planet already would be in the throes of the most violent convulsions, you may be certain.

Man fears the truth and ridicules what it cannot understand. I say to blessed mankind everywhere: AWAKE! THE HOUR HAS COME! Do not listen to the voice of the propagandist, which tries to convince you that there is a better way than the way of Light. Turn to your I AM Presence, the Living Fire of God which made you, and accept the Divine way of life. Saint Germain has warned you, and others have warned you for some time that there was very little time left, and the scoffers and doubters have said: "Well, if a cataclysm were to have occurred why hasn't it occurred as yet?" *It is occurring* even as I speak! The only ones who doubt and scoff are those who have not as yet felt the brunt of that destruction, yet dear ones, it is close upon you.

I say to you—and may these words be branded in your minds with letters of fire—DO NOT DOUBT! DO NOT FEAR! HAVE FAITH IN THE LIGHT OF GOD THAT NEVER FAILS! Do not accept the importance of human things, for they are of passing importance and are of no value when you stand face to face with life. Give! Give! Give! of your love, your substance, your energy, your all, that there may again be a group upon this planet who will hold the reins of destruction in check and bring through into the New Golden Age the Victory and Freedom of Life that has been maintained for this planet for so long. Learn to control your feelings! Learn to control your thoughts! Learn to control your spoken words and your actions! Avoid the appearance of evil! Be true to the Light within you and you will find that the Light will protect its own and you will walk through unharmed when destruction is about you.

You have been taught to give decrees, to face your I AM Presence and pour forth love, and I am grateful that that teaching has come to you, but there are hundreds who, if at the last minute they do not lose their courage and their strength will find themselves moving serenely and calmly through a trembling world amid bursting bombs and fire, untouched and blazing with Light.

The Great Angelic Host, the Legion of Light are joining with this Legion of Freedom upon the planet to protect it and to guide it through into a place of safety, a desired haven.

You may think that I am speaking in a very direful fashion and indeed it may seem so to you and you may scoff or doubt at what I tell you. I will pay no attention to that for I know whereof I speak. O blessed ones, when these laws have been given to you will you not use them? Will you not set aside these human, personal, petty things and live the Law of Love, the law which the great Saviours of humanity have brought to you periodically that you could have the blessing of them? You struggle and fight day after day in seeking to acquire personal things, in seeking to gain physical objects, attention, wealth, position, or some type of compensation, but you do not need to struggle when you pour forth love, dear hearts. The Law of God, the Law of the One, the Law of the I AM is the only way into perfection, and nothing short of perfection will avail at this time.

Humanity must arise and go forward! Humanity has reached the end of a blind alley and must arise and go forward! Too long has blessed, blessed humanity created a new evil just to cure an old one. There is no permanent cure of any evil other than the cure which God alone can bring—the Power and Light from the Mighty I AM. Believe that, for it is true. Doubt it not, and scoff not at that which is real! Accept! O accept! the protection which is at hand for you, that yours may be the power which will draw others into the Light and carry enough of humanity forward into the New Golden Age.

With My Brother, Sanat Kumara, with My Brother, Saint Germain, with My Brother, Jesus, I stand. You will notice that many of mankind will be unable to stand the increase in the rate of vibratory action. You will find that insanity will increase, suicides will increase, and the depravity of mankind will be intensified as the Light grows stronger, for as you know, that which is within the world of the individual is intensified, be it good or bad. Thus you must stand guard, you must accept the great guard that has been established to help you or you cannot be helped. Unless you will accept with your heart, your mind, and all that you have, all the protection which the Arisen Masters have given to you, the Radiation which They bring, then dear ones you are on the outside of that protection and must have the consequences. That protection has been established and will be sustained!

Dear ones, if you "just want to be let alone" you are no student of the Light! If you yourself have a consciousness which demands peace and security at whatever price—if you yourself have the consciousness that is willing to let well enough alone—if yours is a consciousness that will not stand for what you know is right, then dear ones, you have permitted destructive forces to seep into your consciousness and I have great compassion for you.

RISE UP AND TAKE YOUR STAND! You can be firm and loving. You can be powerful and kind. You must be strong and brave and valiant in the hour that has struck for this land. You cannot be weak for humanity needs strength as never before, and the strength of the protection established here shall go to them, make no mistake about it!

With My Heart's Love I pour forth to you My Joy and My Power of Light in action. Accept it and feel your oneness with Me in the days that are to come. Know that no destructive thing has any power to act in your world for *by the Power of the I AM Presence you are above all destruction!* Accept in your feelings these things. You cannot think them through, you must *feel* them through and then you will stand as one to bring in this New Order.

I wish to express My deep gratitude to the blessed students here and elsewhere who have made it possible for My coming. I shall remain working in this solar system until the end of June and you may find many changes taking place between now and then. During this time you have only to speak My Name and I will come to you, and if there is any who thinks that I am not a tangible Being I just ask you to speak My Name and you will know!

My Blessings enfold you now and always.

XVI

GODFRE'S ASCENSION

by Godfre

Blessed ones, as I am with you today I wish to give you just a little picture of the Arisen Masters activity at the Inner levels, for I wish you to have the feeling as well as the understanding of just what it means to be in the Arisen state. Such a short time ago I was in the physical octave as yourselves and oh my! how they did heap it on me sometimes, and sometimes it would look as if I just couldn't rise up out of it. But I always did, because I had the help of Saint Germain and I knew these Great Laws.

Precious ones, the last few days I was never in My physical body, although that stream of Light that connects the physical body of everyone with the I AM Presence remained intact until the Great Ones had all things prepared for Me and then, blessed ones, the joy of finding myself free! Do you know, dear ones, every one of you today present here was present at one time or another during the activity at the Royal Teton, and there, O dear hearts, what a mighty service was rendered to Me!

I wish to tell you a little bit more about it than you have known before, for you have not brought back the conscious memory of it. Saint Germain and Lanto came to Me, one standing on either side, and They conducted Me through that hallway which you have all seen many times, and have had described in *Unveiled Mysteries,* and then We went into the room where the Great Unfed Flame is manifesting at all times. All this time, you understand, I was using a body which Saint Germain had furnished Me, not My Higher Mental Body, but one which He had prepared for this activity. I assure you that I was quite tangible and perfectly aware of everything that was going on. And then, as I stood there, your

Mighty Friend, Victory, together with the Great Divine Director and Sanat Kumara appeared in the atmosphere, and the Light in that room, I tell you precious ones, was *Dazzling*—you cannot conceive of it. I lost all sense of consciousness and seemed to be swimming in a sea of Light, and the raising of the vibratory action must certainly have been felt throughout the planet for the very mountain shook! Beautiful melodies were played and to My senses came the odor of roses and violets. Then suddenly, dear ones, I was in the atmosphere, and through the process which Those far in advance of Myself only know, I was in this Body which had been prepared for Me so long ago and kept there in the casket for just such an activity.

O dear ones, you cannot appreciate the joy and the feeling of love which has sometimes seemed to overwhelm Me since that time. Think of it, dear ones, it was only such a short time ago that I stood in your midst in the physical body and knew with you the limitations, the discords, and O dear Me, so many other things which aren't important at all; and now the Joy and the Freedom to know only Light and to be able to render far greater assistance to Saint Germain and to humanity than ever before. O precious ones, how I have longed to come to you so many times. You know, at first Saint Germain wouldn't let Me. Sometimes I am afraid I pleaded with Him a little too often to just permit Me to come to tell you of the Joy, of the Freedom, of the Love that is in the Arisen state, for dear ones, if you have that firmly within your heart then the outer world has no terror for you at all.

So in coming to you I have released the feeling of My own Victory, which everyone here has gotten so beautifully, some of you more than others, but it has entered into the feeling world of each one and you will long remember this afternoon.

Now blessed ones, do not hesitate to make your dynamic application and do not, I plead with you, let these human disturbing things enter into your worlds again. Just shut them out, for in the Arisen state they do not exist.

Feel My Love and My Blessing flowing to you at all times. O enter into the fullness of your own heart's Light, the Magic Presence, I AM, and there accept the scepter of your dominion. Untouched by any outer disturbing condition, raise yourself quickly into this Perfection which is here. I thank you.

XVII

ALL MANKIND ARE ONE

by Saint Germain

Blessed Children of the Light:

May the full Power of the I AM Presence flow forth to flood your worlds with the fullness of every good and perfect thing, for I come with the greatest Joy and Light yet released to this planet that you may know the great progress which has been made and the Mighty Victory that has been attained!

On this beautiful day has come a great release of Love from the Great Central Sun and it floods the Earth with a quickening consciousness of mankind's responsibility to man, which will begin the task of replacing man's inhumanity to man. This is one of the greatest blessings that has come forth so far, and you will be pleased to know that the strong stand you have taken here has assisted in a very large measure in bringing this about; therefore, you will see how grateful We are for the progress which has been made.

The imperative thing for the student to know is that he does not stand alone. All mankind are one. And that can be understood when the individual enters into the heart of the I AM Presence and there stills himself to become one with the silence, and there recognize his own divinity and pours forth love and blessings to all.

Knowing that mankind all are one is one of the greatest activities which the individual can enter into. The feeling that individuals are separate from their own Source is the thing which causes so many to lose faith, to lack confidence, which otherwise would take them forth to many magnificent victories. You must see that your own confidence is a Power of Light released from the Mighty I AM, and that confidence pouring from you will radiate a similar feeling from you, and thus the Light will expand as a great blessing to any who come within your radiation. As your momentum grows and the activity expands your radiation becomes more and more powerful and you will be able to release greater and greater power for good as you continue.

The privilege that you have in being together in this Focus of Light you do not comprehend except in a very fragmentary fashion, because you see the doubts of so many are so strong in regard to Myself and Others that they cannot accept the great privilege that there is in being here. However, could the human mind be disciplined sufficiently to accept the great privilege you have in being called together under this radiation that you may have the benefit of this instruction and Power of Light released from the Great Central Sun you would very quickly feel the great gratitude which would open the door to oh so many magnificent manifestations for you.

In calling the I AM Presence into action, be absolutely certain that when you wish a definite prompting you visualize yourself held in Light and see that prompting coming to you through its own Wall of Light from the Arisen Masters or from your Presence. Do not accept a prompting which comes to you from the human, and a very quick way to find out if the prompting is from the human or from the Presence is just to ask if you are going to benefit by following that prompting, or if you are going to be rendering a service to bless some one else. The Presence will constantly guide you and the Arisen Masters will constantly release Their radiation to you, provided your desire is always for the higher and the better thing and is for all mankind as well as for yourself. There is nothing wrong with claiming perfection for yourself, but do not mistake that as a prompting—that is a natural thing. When you are calling to receive a prompting from the Presence be certain that the prompting comes from the Presence direct to you on a current of Light and do not accept anything else, because the human, or psychic (and mind you, there is no difference), lies in wait to tell you you have a prompting when it is only a desire.

Watch yourself and when your attention is taken by an appearance do not speak about 'it. Call the Presence into action to take your attention off it. Do not let any human being tell you what you have to do. Call the Presence into action, be loving, be serene, be calm, but give obedience to your I AM Presence and to the promptings which It gives you through your heart, that you may have Harmony, Love, and Happiness in your every activity.

Let Me point out here a very subtle activity that often comes up, for you have heard Me say many times that never should you submit to the domination of individuals and not permit any human being to tell you what you should do. That is very true, but dear ones, at the same time do not refuse to cooperate with individuals who are endeavoring to bring about certain activity. If you want to stand for the Light and Myself you will quickly see that in order to render that service a form must be brought about; order must be maintained, and thus a definite action, and your obligation is to very quickly bring yourself to a point where you are joyfully obedient to the calls of those who are rendering that service. That does not only mean here, but in your work in business, in your homes, or wherever you are.

Remember, you must always listen to the Presence, and that I AM Presence will never, never, never prompt a negative activity. The action of the individual which rebels at authority is just as serious as the individual's willingness to bow to tyranny or dictatorship. Both of those things must be avoided at all cost, and unless the individual understands he can call to the Presence and receive a definite, clear answer on all occasions, he cannot possibly have the sustaining power in his own world that will see him through any and every situation.

Blessed ones, in your activity remember you stand as the way showers to those who do not know this Law from the physical standpoint, just exactly as the Arisen Masters stand as the way showers to you who do know the Law. Remember, no matter who you contact or what discordant activity may seem to be acting in their world, your obligation is to love and bless them, not to see the imperfection, not to condemn or judge, but to help by pouring forth your love and blessings.

How mankind loves the individual who is capable of pouring forth love. How mankind longs for the law which will permit each one to turn to his own God Presence again and recognize the Oneness of all things. Humanity has strayed so long and so far from the Great Divine Truths of Life that they have reached their rope's end and are crying desperately for something to which to cling. This Truth and this Light is the life saving action to humanity, for this Truth and this Light is not dependent upon human beings but is going forward through the principles that have been released through the activity of the calls of the students everywhere and the activity of this Focus that has been established. This Truth and this Light shall enfold the planet!

Your heart, which is the anchoring place of your Presence, will tell you what the perfect thing for you shall be. Know always that as you turn to that I AM Presence and accept Its Blazing Light, Its Mighty Omnipresent Reality, you have entered the realm of the Arisen Masters and stand at-one with the Great God Presence of Life, the Mighty I AM.

Do not hesitate to call the Presence into action to release into your hands and use that which you require for your greater blessing. If you never use that activity selfishly, but call it forth to be a great blessing, a blessing to others, then you will never have to retract a statement. You will never have to turn around and go back to find where the mistake has occurred. Remember, if you will always seek to learn what more you can do to assist others you will never have reason to be sorry or to regret any action, speech or feeling that you may release.

Man needs so much the activity and the understanding of love, for unless the blessed children of Earth realize that love is the substance of all life, and life itself is God, the Mighty I AM, then how in the world are they going to have the strength and the courage that comes only with the absolute knowledge of that reality which will see them through the coming changes.

At this point I wish to bring to your attention one of the Laws which We have said very little about lately and yet it is something that you must remember. Dear ones, in order for Us to have an activity in the outer world We must of necessity depend upon human channels. That is absolutely essential, and by channels I am referring to all of you, for each one of you represents Myself and the Arisen Host. Each one of you must, therefore, be strong enough and powerful enough and earnest enough to follow the instructions which come through from Myself and the others of the Great Host of Light.

There is a certain activity of the human consciousness which, when a statement is made by an Arisen Master or by one or another of the Arisen Host, instead of accepting the truth intended in the statement, the human instantly desires to test that truth to see if it is absolutely so. Now you will understand that in the activity of life there are many things which appear to be a perfect paradox and thus you will see while many times I will tell you one thing, you can from the human standpoint turn around and say: just a little while ago I said exactly the opposite. That is what has happened many times and blessed ones have turned aside from this Light for they have failed to accept the truth which was given but have instead sought to find some flaw whereby they could reject the truth.

Now I am not telling you this to get you off your guard or to just make you accept without calling your Presence into action, but for goodness sakes call your Presence into action and do not just reject merely for the sake of argument. That is something you will have to watch very closely because there is quite a momentum in the outer world that when a statement is made it is not accepted but it is tested by the human intellect to see if perhaps it can be torn apart. Now that is a fine thing in some ways regarding the human but it does not work in regard to the Divine Law. If you heart is shut against that truth We cannot help you and you will find if you will accept the Truth which We give you, you will be happier, more radiant, more prosperous, more victorious in everything you do.

And by the way, I wish to say to you blessed ones in business, do not hesitate to call to Me in your business activity. I am quite interested in assisting you in the success of your business. If you will call to Me to assist you in the service that you are performing, in your position, whatever it may be, asking to be guided correctly that you always do the perfect thing and render the perfect service, you will receive a great deal of assistance which otherwise will not be coming to you. Do not feel that I am above the service to humanity through business channels for I am not, and it might interest you to know that the Blessed Master Jesus and Myself have worked a great deal in the business avenues throughout this land and throughout the world for quite a number of years. Now if We can expend a little attention and a little energy in that direction, surely you must realize that there is a great purpose in it, so do not hesitate to call for assistance in that direction.

To return to this matter of acceptance, remember dear ones, the human loves to argue. The human loves to elevate itself or expound its mental achievements. The student of Light and the Master loves to learn the Truth and, therefore, is a willing receptacle to the Light pouring forth from the Great Host of Light. Only the human rejects. The Master who gives all receives all. If you wish to receive you will first learn to give, for giving is the whole of the Law applied. I do not mean there to give of discord, but to give of Arisen Master qualities and Arisen Master activities.

XVIII

THE LAW OF THE ATTENTION

by Saint Germain

Beloved Students of Light and Seekers after Truth:

This afternoon We are trying something that We have not attempted for some time, and while this activity is going on and this Blessed Boy is reading these Words which I am flashing before him, the consciousness of everyone within the sound of his voice will be raised very perceptibly. Therefore, dear ones, I wish you to feel absolutely at ease, and please understand that although this activity which is taking place may seem to you a little bit unusual, there is nothing in it of the hypnotic or spiritualistic state in any way and you may believe that whatever words come forth are charged with Light and Love for your blessing, so you may accept them with your full heart.

Understand, dear ones, that it is the radiation of the Arisen Master which means so much to the student, and unless the student is placed in a position where he can at first hand receive that radiation, then there will always be a greater amount of doubt acting in his world.

The Great Goddess of Peace has been enthroned in the atmosphere over San Francisco and Her Rays of Light and Love have been pouring forth rendering a transcendent service. Those of you who have turned your attention to Her consciously and sent Her your love and blessing have assisted very greatly. It is her intention, shall sufficient harmony come about, to come into the physical octave, and while remaining invisible, still to lower Her Tangible Presence into Washington, D.C., London, Berlin, Tokyo, and other centers, there releasing Her Feeling of Peace. Before it is possible for Her to lower Her Tangible form into the physical octave, a place that would remain harmonious long enough had to be found, and We feel that with the attention of the blessed ones here being focused upon the Light and the sincere calls being made, that the way has opened sufficiently and within the next few hours the attempt will be made.

I wish to go into a certain explanation concerning the Inner Realms of Light, for it is quite apparent to Me that there is a feeling in the worlds of several that no physical object can be affected in any way by those who manifest only at the Inner levels, and I wish definitely to assure you that the Council Chamber at the Royal Teton, and My Home at Table Mountain, Chananda's Home, the Secret Valley, also the Retreat at Mount Shasta, and many other places, are real physical places and exist both at the outer and Inner levels. We do not admit individuals in their physical bodies, but they do occupy physical space, and I wish you to understand that unmistakably. Also, many of the records which are held at the Royal Teton and elsewhere are tangible, physical records—three dimensional objects, dear ones. Those are the records which have been saved and protected and will be released at the conclusion of this period of change.

I wish you to understand that the Arisen Masters, or yourselves working at the Inner levels unascended, are quite capable of handling physical objects. Remember dear ones, at the Inner levels you are above the human and, therefore, you are master of it as well as being master of the next plane of consciousness. I trust that you will get this for your understanding of these laws and your balance and your love in expressing them will surely raise the planet as you continue on.

As you rise in consciousness you naturally master all things which are beneath you. Thus it is that mankind, having free will and being created in the image of God the Father, the Mighty I AM, has dominion over all things created with free will and with the I AM Presence as the Directing Intelligence. Thus you will see why it is that man had dominion over the Earth and all that is within it, had dominion over the elements and the forces of the elements, until he proved that he was unable to control his feelings and his thoughts, and then these lower things took dominion over him. Thus you will quickly see that storms, earthquakes, fires, and floods are nothing more nor less than man's self generated discord.

Now dear ones, call to the I AM Presence and to the Blessed Master, the Venetian, to assist in releasing the quality of patience to you, and also, don't forget to call to Beloved Godfre in that respect, for His activity has been very largely the expressing of patience. Train yourselves to hold your physical body still, and then when you move it have a reason, a clear direction for the movement. Learn to hold your energy in check and then release it only when you wish to accomplish a definite purpose. That way you will develop poise, self confidence, God dominion, and express the Victory of Life.

Have patience with one another, and when you find that there is some one who seems to have the power to disturb you in any way, remember that the activity of disturbance in your world could only have come about because of your willingly directed attention. Therefore, instantly take your attention from the disturbing element, place it back on your Presence, and rejoice that you have been cut free from any disturbing condition whatsoever. I assure you the law of the attention cannot be over emphasized!

Another thing I should like to say to you is this: Do not feel in calling to the I AM Presence that physical effort is needed. Feel rather that sincerity is the human requirement. You must enter into the silence, into the heart of your Presence, and there feel the full power of that Light which is the Great I AM within you and accept Its Mighty Radiation, Its Mighty Power of Light pouring through you. That is a perfectly natural activity and will always be beneficial. You can be absolutely certain that nothing discordant, inharmonious or negative ever in any way comes from the Presence of God, therefore, have no fear in calling the Presence into action and asking for Its Dominion in your world and in the world and affairs of your Nation.

It is imperative that you understand that your calls to the I AM Presence are all that is needed to take you from the human into the divine. It is not necessary to pass judgment, to criticize, to condemn; it is not necessary to feel that you are either inferior or superior to some other human being. Instead, if you will abide within the Great Presence of Life, the Mighty I AM, you will have Its blessing released through you and your world in an ever expanding activity.

No longer permit lethargic forces to take control of your mind, your body, your feelings! Stand on your feet and release your energy, and if you should make a few mistakes, that is far better than no application!

Mankind needs to be awakened! I wish you to understand the human consciousness is like a caged animal. The human consciousness, to get its desire will tear apart like a tiger tearing at a piece of meat. It makes no difference who it may be, your human is something that is far from constructive. You yourself are divine. The I AM Presence, the Great Light which beats your heart, is the substance of Light itself, the divinity of all life everywhere present, but the human, which is the outer consciousness, is the great enemy of mankind.

I want you to realize the human is a very cunning, a very clever little fellow, for the human will suggest to you every logical excuse why you should not do something; why you should not make your application; why you should stand and wait for miracles; why you should doubt the Arisen Masters. That is the activity of the human, but the human is telling you nothing but lies when it tells you those things! You must stand supreme in your own world and refuse acceptance of those suggestions, for as long as you give them power in your world you will have discord acting. Doubt and fear are the things that limit mankind, and until doubt and fear are driven from your world, dissolved and transmuted by the Violet Transmuting Flame, you will have them acting for they are what drive man into discord, inharmony, death and destruction. Doubt and fear alone are responsible, but because they have been generated by man they will act until he has thrown them out.

In your calls to the Presence you stand Supreme! When you say: *"I AM Presence come forth, sweep into action here,"* you release the Power of the Universe to flood forth to fulfill your command. When you call the Presence into action and stand at-one with Its Radiance and Power of Light you make it possible for your world to be cleansed and purified and raised out of all things human. But so long as you desire human things you will have them, for your desire world is a barometer of what is registering in your world. Call: *"Beloved I AM Presence, cleanse and purify my desires. See that I desire only Thy Perfection and the Perfection of the Arisen Masters."* Say also: *"I AM the Presence of pure desire filling my world and the world of every human being everywhere."*

There is so often a desire on the part of the student to lean upon some other student or to look to some other human being that very often the student robs himself of the progress which he might otherwise make. Blessed ones, stand your ground! Do not permit these negative forces to drive in and take possession of you even for an instant, and when you feel yourself impelled to do or say some negative thing, instantly get away from human beings and call on the Fire of Forgiveness and use the Violet Transmuting Flame with tremendous activity so that you will not be responsible for an act which will eventually come back to you. If you will only learn that what you release comes back, then you will not release these things of inharmony and imperfection. You can govern your world, you are the only one who can, and you must do it!

If you wish to live in a world of harmony, happiness, beauty, and perfection you will see that the simple rule to obtain that is by conquering your human, for in disciplining yourself never to pour forth anything but the highest of vibratory action, in its return to you, you will be blessed. No longer let the human have any power to dominate or control you. Instead, take your stand in the great Oneness of the Presence of Life, the Mighty I AM. Refuse acceptance of human conditions and let your Light so shine as to illumine all darkness everywhere!

* * *

Dear ones, you stand today at the open doorway of the Corridor of Time, for Earth and its people have reached the place where Cosmic Time begins, and you who stand with the conscious knowledge of the I AM Presence and the Arisen Host and with the great momentum of application behind you, stand at this open doorway which will serve to usher all of mankind into the presence of the Arisen Host and their own victory.

You have been told many times that happiness is the highest rate of vibratory action in the universe, and so it is, for true happiness cannot act until all other Arisen Master qualities are also manifesting in a measure. Now then it would naturally seem to you that the achievement of happiness would be the greatest goal for any individual to seek, however, may I prompt you to remember that happiness, unless it is arrived at through love, through generosity, and through a complete putting away of human desire, is not happiness at all but rather the satisfaction of the human consciousness, the sensation of physical experience, or the attainment of physical pleasure. Now these two things, happiness and pleasure, while appearing to be similar are as far apart as the poles. One is the activity of the divinity, the other is the activity of the human, and in your search for happiness, which naturally is what all mankind is searching for, do not be misled into the pathway of pleasure. You must be balanced and happy in all things that you do.

Another thing I wish to call to your attention is that you should remember the law concerning pity and compassion. When an individual has disobeyed the law and then reaction of that disobedience sets in, as it surely will, please, blessed ones, if you wish yourself to be free, do not in any way become sorry for that individual because when you do you open yourself to the destruction and you don't help him in the least. When you observe some individual who is reaping the results of his own wrong desire, make the call to the Presence, call on the Fire of Forgiveness, ask for the individual's blessing and then take your attention off the appearance and know that God only is acting in that one. Should he come to you with a very sad story about the situation, listen, call forth a blessing, call on the Fire of Forgiveness for the individual and for yourself, and dismiss it. Do not hold it in your consciousness! If you do, I tell you just as surely as there is a Great Presence of Life, you will draw those destructive things into your world and you will have to handle them, and instead of assisting one who seems to be in need of assistance you will be amplifying his own discord and making it worse for him.

Do not, I plead with you, fall into the mistaken idea of pity. Many people tell you they have a very soft heart, but the truth of the matter is they have a very soft head, and they should stand their ground very firmly and be positive. Now that doesn't mean you have to be cruel, cold, or abrupt. You can be kind and loving and make the call for anyone at any time, but please do not be imposed upon by individuals who are determined to tell you all sorts of sad and unjust things. When you run across such individuals who cannot be avoided, be firm with them. You know the old story of the Mother and her son walking with the other boys—they were all out of step but him. Well, it just doesn't work that way, as you know.

In this same matter of understanding the activities between the two sexes, male and female, I should like you to understand that one of the tools of the sinister force for centuries has been the silly romantic notions that young people fall into. Now I know some of you are going to think I am an old fossil for telling you that but I think I know what I am talking about because there wasn't anybody who had more work to do on his own human than I did in that connection. You see, dear ones, the danger point is reached when either the young boy or the young girl begins to look upon the opposite one as being a special piece of property for himself or herself, for when that feeling of possession sets in nothing short of an explosion will chase it out, and you may be certain that the explosion will arrive in due time.

If only mankind would awaken to the fact that divine love is the eternal essence of life and must be poured forth, not just to one individual but to all individuals, what a heaven on Earth would manifest that day! There is nothing in the world so limiting to the individual's expansion as his tying himself to another human personality. Dear ones, I wish you to understand this completely. Every individual has his own I AM Presence, which is the Supreme Source of all life, and to that I AM Presence he or she can turn and receive limitless direct assistance. The mistaken idea that the individual has to turn and lean on some other human personality is one of the things which has caused a lack of application on the part of a great, great number of people, and a dominating activity on the part of another great number. You may be positively certain that your ascension in the Light and your complete and final victory depends upon your own calls to your Presence, and you do not make your ascension with some one else, you make it by yourself! Sooner or later every human being must face that fact. You come into the world alone, and you go out of physical embodiment alone, and when you have achieved your mastery you rise into the fullness of your Presence, alone.

I am saying this with all the love and kindness in the world, but I wish you to understand it unmistakably for it is these things that bind humanity upon the cross of suffering generation after generation; bind and limit themselves through the foolish idea that there isn't any other way. The Arisen Masters' way is the other way, and for all those who have tried it, it is by far the best, as anyone who knows anything about it can tell you.

How We rejoice when We find the individual, whoever he or she may be, putting aside the human ties that bind and turning to God, the I AM Presence, and saying: *"Into Thy Hands my Father do I give all things."* Then the joy, the happiness of the Arisen Masters octave is made manifest to the individual and, dear ones, not until. As long as the individual persists in placing some other human being or some activity before his own Presence he will never know the

Glory and Splendor, the Beauty and Perfection of the Inner realms of Light.

Those of you who have tried this know whereof I speak, and those of you who have not as yet had the magnificent experience, will you not do as I have suggested. Go by yourself and call your I AM Presence into action, asking to be cut free from every human being, and make no exceptions in your mind, no mental reservations. Call to your Presence to be cut free from every human being, from every human tie, then stand facing your own God self and asking for that Light to pour down in and through you and say: *"Thou I AM, Thou Supreme Source of all Life, I acknowledge only Thee and give to Thy keeping my life, my energy, my substance, which is really Thine. Henceforth there is only Thee."* Blessed ones, when you will do that you will find such great joy.

I do not mean by what I have said now that the individual should feel free, after making that call, just to run around and forget about his obligations or anything of the sort, nor do I mean in any way that the individual should become an outcast and refuse to associate with his fellow beings, but the ties that bind, dear ones, are different than the ties of love, and you have every right to call the Presence into action to sever the ties that bind and replace them by ties of love, that you never limit or hinder in any way. You must take your positive, strong stand in this matter and let no human being interfere with the fulfillment of your call. Call to your Presence that you may be a being of love alone and accept that your I AM Presence is quite capable of establishing that activity in your world now and forever.

Mankind everywhere is longing oh with such intensity for the explanation of the Laws of Life which you know, and yet it is perfectly amazing, they wouldn't for a minute accept that explanation if you were to make it to them. However, your actions, your own life, can be the example to them which they so much desire, for you who have stood together here thus far so beautifully in such a precious way are making many things possible, for often when you know it not, individuals receive a great deal of assistance from you and you don't know a thing about it.

Dear ones, you must realize that life, the I AM Presence, is no hard taskmaster. Life, the living of life in the understanding of your own God self is only the natural, the beautiful way to live and there is nothing about the living of life which should in any way appear to be hard, cold, or set, for life, if you are to live it correctly from the Arisen Masters' standpoint must be lived with a constant expansion of your activity, a constant widening vision, and you cannot have that if you allow yourself to get into a rut, into the old habit of going on from day to day and never looking upward and outward.

Virtue is its own reward. When you as an individual live the Law of Love, the Law of Life, and turn your attention to the I AM Presence and the Great Beings Who stand ever ready to assist you, you do not need to have proof of the reality of that Presence or the Great Ones for the proof is instantly in your own world as a result of the radiation, as a result of the action which you automatically will have and experience.

Be loyal and true to the Light as you carry it, and do not, I plead with you, doubt the wisdom of the Great Ones who govern, guide and direct the destinies of men. Even though there may be many things you do not understand; even though there may be many things you may outwardly be inclined to question, do not do it, I plead with you. Just accept the Power of Light that knows no opposite. Stand by your I AM Presence and go forward. Thus you will enjoy the true essence of Victory and will live above all human things.

From the Brotherhood of the Royal Teton, the Brotherhood of Mount Shasta, the Brotherhood of Yosemite, from Diana of Mount Tamalpais, from Urlando, the Goddess of Wisdom, the Goddess of Justice, the Great Divine Director, Khubal Kumara, Sanat Kumara, from your own Precious Godfre, and the many serving the humanity of Earth as it battles back and forth, I bring you greetings, Love and Blessings. Accept them. Know what they mean and then, dear hearts, bestir yourselves as never before. Leap to the task of conquering yourself. Rejoice that you are free!

XIX

MAN MOVES ON A HIGHER SPIRAL

by Cyclopea

The Arisen Host is making intensive preparation for the great Conclave to be held at the Royal Teton at the end of this year. For the first time in many years I have been chosen to preside at that meeting, and you may be very sure that the activities to be accomplished over this new period of time will be transcendent beyond your fondest dreams. The appearance of discordant feelings, inharmony, and imperfection which still pervade this planet are being dissolved and consumed with the speed of Light. The release of the Great Cosmic Light flooding forth now filling every nook and cranny of the earth is bringing about an awareness of the great reality of life, the I AM Presence.

Under a dispensation made some time ago it became possible for individuals to make the ascension even though their bodies were not raised far enough so that they could take the physical body with them into the higher octave. This you already know. Another dispensation has now come forth making it possible that constructive individuals, when they have arrived at the conclusion of their earthly pilgrimage, not only will have an opportunity of going forth into the higher octaves, but will have the personal assistance of one or another of the Great Arisen Masters helping to raise the vibratory action of the being and world of the individual to a point where reembodiment will never be necessary again. I wish to assure you this activity is very real and very powerful, and there are many whom you know who have already been blessed in this fashion.

Blessed ones, since My activity to the Earth is the representation of the All Seeing Eye of God, it is only natural that I bring you some of the information which you have been curious about. In spite of the appearance on this planet, you have My assurance that war has ceased for this planet, and for all time! Remember that. There are still forces that are loose seeking to embroil this country against that country, one group against another. Those forces have no power! Their guiding and directing intelligence is no longer present, and peace will reign again upon this Earth! Even as it did before in the second Golden Age, will it come a third time, and this time to remain. Make no mistake about it, this is being done, even tonight as I speak. Great cosmic activities are taking place now. One will follow so quickly upon the heels of the former one that even those unillumined individuals still inhabiting your Earth will become aware of the fact that there must be some great, transcendent, wonderful, pure expression of life beyond their knowledge; and once the unillumined portion of mankind can be made aware that something beyond their consciousness exists, your way will be much easier.

I charge you, have no fear! Stand your guard! Call your I AM Presence into action! Release this Law! Tell humanity the truth concerning their own relationship to God! Let the children of Earth know that they are children of Light! Teach them, young and old alike. Let your hearts rejoice, with Saint Germain and Others who have guided you through the years.

Mankind is reaching a point in its progress where the recognition of these great Truths take it forward into a period of perfection, the like of which has not been seen on this Earth for thousands of years, in fact, has never been seen, because this time mankind goes forward on a higher spiral and activity of life.

Once again must I assure you that there is no death. There is only a change of form, and I assure you that everyone who has ever been present with you is present with you now—now and always. Progress continues. That raising of the consciousness makes possible newer and brighter days, greater and greater perfection pouring forth. Those who have finished service in one form take up a greater service in another. In serving you go forward. Feel and accept this for it is the very truth of life and your hearts know and respond to that truth as it pours forth to you.

The Arisen Masters are real and soon mankind will know Their reality, for here and there across the face of the globe enlightened individuals will come face to face with the Arisen Masters, recognize them as their Elder Brothers, and be shocked into Their way of life from that moment on.

Accept the power of this Light! Accept the conscious-ness of your I AM Presence emblazoned in your mind as never before! Feel, accept the power of the All Seeing Eye of God, and know that I am with you at all times, working now with this planet as it has not been possible to work with it for some time. Accept the activity of the coming Conclave, which, as you have already been told, will last for five days, and know that your activity in this physical octave is the outpicturing of what We are performing on the Inner levels. Prepare for and be ready on an instant's notice to let flow forth Arisen Master miracles of Love, Wisdom, and Perfection.

XX

THE COSMIC HOUR

by The Mighty Elohim Arcturus

I have come forth from Cosmic space, blessed students of the one Truth, as a result of the time, the place, and the condition being correct for My coming. Saint Germain and Others of your Arisen Brothers have long asked Me to come forth to set into motion this new activity which Saint Germain has brought into being. I have not come forth at His request, but have come forth instead as a result of the striking of the Cosmic Hour, the creation of the proper condition, and the bringing together at the proper place those who are ready to dedicate their lives that this Truth concerning man's origin, man's destiny, and his rightful place and function upon this planet be made known.

There are many with Me here this evening who have come forth from the Inner realms of Light, and as I am conducting this program with you there will take place at the Inner levels at a distance of some three thousand feet above this exact spot a ceremony of Inner significance which will later be revealed to you.

For what has seemed to you many long years you have attempted sincerely and earnestly to do the Arisen Master bidding. Often the way has seemed dark. Many times the activity of human consciousness, the mental appearance or impression, has created a situation of confusion, doubt, or fear, yet you have risen above those things and gone on, seeking ever in your heart to be the fulfillment of the Law as Saint Germain has given it to you.

Blessed ones, the reward for your strong stand is at hand in that which is taking place above you at the Inner levels at this time. Each one of you is receiving additional strength and additional courage which is radiating to you with tremendous power. This strength and courage will cause you to stand unswervingly for the Light, for the Truth, for that which you know is right, regardless of the comments or the discussions of individuals who are unable to harmonize their feelings.

The reality of the Arisen Host of Light is a reality which mankind will now accept! Have no fear concerning the explanations of these laws. I charge each one of you with the responsibility of seeing that these laws are given forth; that the explanation goes forth in clear, concise terms, and that the understanding of these laws is complete.

In calling to your individualized focus of life which you are, you will feel that great power always comes by using the words "I AM" for this is God's Name; however, I wish to assure you that *there is no magic in the use of any word or any group of words. The magic is in your heart,* not in the word. In using the words—I AM, God self, Individualized Flame of Life, or any other such term which indicates your own divinity, the use of the words themselves is only a small part of the release of the necessary light and energy which will bring about the result that you desire. Make your calls, whatever terms you use, with feeling and with conviction. Accept the reality of this great Presence which you are; accept it, and pour forth the acceptance of it that others, in absorbing your feeling, will learn to accept also.

Take your attention from human beings, for the activity of this Light concerns you from a divine standpoint and not from a human standpoint.

Taking place in the atmosphere above you now is a most magnificent and gorgeous activity which I will describe to you. There is a great oval approximately three thousand feet overhead, and around this oval facing outward are fifty great Devas. Above them at a higher level stand the Cherubim and Seraphim, one at either end of the oval. Moving continuously in and out, swerving around, are many Angels, the rays of Light and the color of Their beings making a splendid display of beauty. Higher still, and presiding over this activity are four Great Cosmic Masters—the Great Divine Director, Sanat Kumara, the Silent Watcher, and Khubal Kumara. The radiation from this great oval, which is very nearly a mile in length, is pouring down to drench this City and to assist you in that which you are to do. There are many in this location tonight who will feel the reality of their great God self as they have never felt it before and who will accept the great spiritual impact of Light for the first time.

I caution you not to judge from the human appearance, for if you do not judge you will see only perfection, the perfection which flows from the level of the Masters, and the perfection which will cause you to rise with Them into that beauty, harmony, and the at-one-ment which is your goal.

I charge you never to doubt for a minute the activity of the Arisen Masters! I charge you never to doubt for a minute your own divinity! I charge you never to doubt for a minute that great and perfect connection which exists now and for all time between Us and you!

The Cosmic Hour has struck for this planet when inharmony and discord shall cease! When I uttered those words the other evening, setting aside all previous dispensations, some of you did not quite realize all that took place at that moment. I have intervened to establish on this Earth the activity of Truth and Light explained to mankind, that they may come to know and understand the reality of life and move forward in harmony and cooperation with that reality. Human beings have gone on their way constantly determined to set all natural laws at naught, to do as they pleased selfishly, to satisfy their own desires and appetites. The time has come when individuals desiring to follow selfish pathways will not have the sustaining force to go on with that type of activity!

Humanity must learn to live for one another. This, dear ones, applies not only to those of humanity here in the United States of America but to the humanity of this planet wherever they may be, of whatever color or creed, of whatever doctrine or habit—*the humanity of this planet will come into divine order,* and that has been decreed by Us! The out-picturing will come about through your own earnest application.

I wish to explain certain things to you which have been a matter of some concern to all of you from time to time. First, the activity of these Laws must be conducted in perfect naturalness. Dear ones, though these Truths which have been given to you and are being given to you constantly are of deep spiritual importance, you may not, in your activity concerning them, be hypocritical or appear in any way to be especially holy or untouchable. These laws which have been given to you are practical and are intended for practical application. Your activity, though you will have great spiritual impact, must be presented naturally, simply, sincerely. There is nothing spiritualistic or occult, there is nothing mystifying or peculiar about these laws. The peculiar thing and the mystifying thing is that humanity has refused to accept these laws even though they recognize them in their hearts as being so. You will remove that peculiarity and that mystery in your work. *You are so charged!*

There has been a great deal of confusion and misconception concerning the activity of sex as presented under previous dispensations. I wish to clarify some of these things at this time. The activity of sex is an activity closely related to each individual's own spiritual power. An individual who persists in sexual practices which drain his or her energies merely for the purpose of gratification is disobeying one of God's highest laws and the end is always sure. Now, dear ones, this does not mean that there is anything wrong in the practice of sexual relationship when it takes place under certain specific conditions. That activity was intended as a natural function, there is nothing wrong with it under the laws of God, and according to the present stage of humanity. Such practices may occur only between married people and only for the purpose of giving birth, giving new bodies to individuals coming forth to render their service here.

I wish you to understand thoroughly that *the activity of your lives here on this planet is for the purpose of serving God and humanity* and not for the purpose of self-indulgence, the satisfaction of appetites, greed, lust, etc. I wish to make this point emphatically clear because it is very important that those who come to you in future be given this understanding. It is very important that beloved young people understand that there is nothing wrong with marriage, that there is nothing wrong with the activity of having children, that as a matter of fact there are great illumined beings waiting to reembody who can only reembody with parents who are spiritually informed. It is necessary for bodies to be furnished these blessed ones who will help to raise humanity, and I assure you that there is nothing wrong with that activity at this particular stage of this planet. May I again repeat, however, and lay emphasis upon the fact that sexual practices for any other reason than the reason mentioned are wilful disobedience of God's law and will lead slowly but surely to dissolution and decay.

The activity of life, dear ones, is not an activity from which you can escape, because you are a part of life. You exist in the universe as a part of the universe. You cannot escape from it for there is nowhere else that you may go. You are, therefore, subject to the Laws of the Universe. If you follow these laws you will find peace, harmony, happiness, prosperity, understanding, friendship, and all of those beautiful perfect activities coming into your world making your world indeed a garden of perfection. If, on the other hand, you persist in allowing the human appetites to govern your thoughts and feelings you will find yourself giving vent on occasion to violent bursts of temper; you will find things arising over which you have no control; you will find that your world is in confusion, that doubts and fears enter in, and instead of being master you will find yourself in the process of being controlled by outside forces. These things have no power over you as an individual who faces the one God, who recognizes that divinity within himself and is true to that divinity at all times.

I wish also to say in connection with this same subject We are speaking of that it is not possible for individuals to stop certain habits just by the use of sheer will power. It is neither possible nor wise for the activity of human consciousness, of human will, to be given dominion over an individual.

Beloved students of Truth, know this for all time: The activity of God comes about in God's own way. Make your application and accept the result as being present now, complete, then do not set the human will or the human consciousness to watch over that call to see how quickly the result does arrive. I tell you the result is already there before you have made the call. If you do not see its outpicturing, that is because of your own limited vision, your own lack of conception of what it means when We say there is no time or space, that there is no power that can stand between you and the immediate fulfillment of every command you make in the Name of Almighty God, your own self.

Blessed ones, if you comprehend even for a few moments that which I have told you this evening, your freedom and your mastery is at hand.

Note:

The Elohim are the Great Builders. The name "Elohim" explains the trinity of action of all life, shows the masculine and feminine elements working in conjunction, and indicates the power of creation through the I AM Presence. The name "Elohim" is one of the most powerful names which can be uttered or held in mind. It literally means God in Action through His creation expanding Himself. The seven Great and Mighty Ones who have earned the title of "Elohim" are the builders of this Universe and work with systems of planets.

XXI

THE I AM PRESENCE

by The Presence

Say: "I AM the Presence right here, right now! I AM that Presence." Visualize yourself as a Light that is pulsating, that is of the rhythmic pulsebeat, and about yourself see the Causal Body. That body, in physical words, does not come and go, nor is it moving. It is a permanent thing about you. Its brilliancy is beyond description in the human; the power of it is beyond human comprehension, and all the functions of that accumulated energy of the Seven Rays is beyond understanding and description to the mind on the human plane because it is a function of a higher plane. However, as you tune in to it and one of your senses picks up, either by sight or feeling or comprehension, you have a faint glimpse or understanding of this power, its reality and function, its specific purpose. But for the sake of lifting yourself into the Presence, for the sake of doing away with the feeling of separateness from your own God self, just accept that you can see this Causal Body, accept that you can feel it.

If you do not know what to visualize, ask that in some way you can comprehend something tangible that permits, that forces every atom of your being to see, feel, hear, and grasp the reality of the Causal Body about you. Remember, the Causal Body is all good. It is your accumulated good which you have accumulated all through the ages, and since it is all good, it is of a high vibratory action. It is Love you have given unselfishly. It is Wisdom, Kindness, Joy, Happiness, Peace, Purity, Freedom, Light, all the things you have released which are good.

In order for that to be drawn to you and you into that great Power, you have to clear yourself from the misqualified energy. Such misqualified energy is dark, muddy, murky looking in color. It is of a low vibratory rate and acts as a weight about you. The Fire of Forgiveness transmutes and is of a vibratory rate that lifts and purifies. You not only have to clear from your consciousness thoughts and understanding of this low misqualified energy, you have to remove it from your thoughts, feelings, and vision so that you can put in its place this sheer beauty of the Body of the Presence that you are. The Fire of Forgiveness can do this work for you.

In order for that complete I AM Consciousness to take dominion, all else must get out of your world. Can you grasp that? See yourself as that Sun, then see the Sun expand in its Light with a vengeance, with a great force, with great power pushing behind it just like it says: "I shall now clean out your world and no longer can darkness or density exist ever again." See it just blaze out from you and clear away all things dark, all confusion and chaos, and then as the Light takes residence in your form, your aura, then about you see that great ball consisting of the colors of the Seven Planes, your accumulated good, and then take the consciousness: "I AM the Presence." You are the Presence right here where you are now!

Now if you have followed that you have changed your consciousness, for stepping into the great I AM Consciousness permanently is a matter of changing your thoughts and feelings. It is as simple as that. It is the thin veil that is referred to; but you will remember what I said right in the very beginning: the most powerful thing you can do is for you to accept and affirm, be and understand that *"I AM the Presence right here and now!* It is right here. It is not away any place else, it is for me. *I AM the Presence."* As you say it, visualize it! Do it again and again and again! Do it while you are walking, before you go to sleep, and when you awaken. Then the heart is the center, the source of all in-come. And the heart pours unto the mind, the brain, that magnificent faculty, the things which are to be accomplished.

The brain is the man at the helm. The brain is the man at the wheel. The brain is the director of this wonderful energy; but your source, your ideas, your in-flow is in your heart. It is the hub upon which your entire system revolves. Each part of your body is a function and some of the parts have a very large function. It consists of many intelligent cells that have specific work. But most magnificent outside of the heart is that which fills the center of the brain.

The first thing that is illumined in the physical form as illumination takes place is the brain. The brain cells are the first to be raised. They have to raise first before the body can be illumined or raised into the next state of consciousness. Therefore, the Light that comes into the heart, and the distribution point in your body immediately back of the heart, sets up a wonderful action on this plane of consciousness, and in the process of your own individual lifting or expanding, this magnificent Light deposits a wonderful and secret substance into the brain; so think often: *"I AM the complete illumination of my brain."*

Your mind is a section of the brain operation. Your will is a section of the brain operation. Your Cosmic Understanding is a section of the brain operation, but combined it all must raise, so say often: *"I AM Cosmic Understanding. I AM the complete illumination of my brain center,"* and speak directly to your brain center, via your heart, and say: *"Awaken every cell in my brain."* But you must do this from the heart into this magnificent function otherwise you would be talking from your mind to your mind and would not pick up the substance. You can follow through on the Light which comes from the Godhead, and remember, as you take the consciousness: *I AM the Presence,* you become the Presence; therefore, when you then enter deeper into the inner realms you dip into the substance that comes from within, or above, or for the sake of visualizing or feeling, accept that you are drawing this substance from the Central Sun, or the Heart of God, Creation, or the Source of the Infinite, whatever you wish to call it.

Remember, as that comes down then from the Great Source as a thin stream of Light, or a gigantic stream of Light, whichever helps you to visualize it, see its function go into the heart for your own individual advancement, and lifting, see that return Light returning back to the Great Source and like a great rope of Light pulling you ever upward. That is your own individual growth; also the lifting of the physical form, the great function that transpires in your form from the head through the throat center, through the alimentary canal and solar plexus center and into the kundalini in the back, up the spine center and into the pituitary gland, that intertwines with the other circle of Light that is above, and the two are the thing that causes action transpiring in your form. It causes, you would say, the two poles to act, positive and negative. It is the thing that pours in and pushes out, or causes you to close and expand. It is all those forces that are the operation of the Universe, and you yourself function in the same manner on a smaller scale.

If in meditation you can see this and desire to know more about it, there you will receive the operation of this magnificent Light more than can be put into physical words. It is very hard to explain it. You often ask why do not the channels give more instruction as to how these centers function so we can further advance ourselves, but it is something that you must get yourself. It is identical to the Master cannot breathe for you, nor can He eat or think for you, nor can He ascend for you—that you must do yourself, and so it is in understanding the functioning of your own magnificent form. It is the greatest miracle on Earth in the physical plane, the function of the human temple. You all have been shown this activity many times but in trying to see it as an actual picture and understanding it from the outer means of understanding, such as books, drawings, etc., you failed to grasp the delicate way your Presence shows the steps of understanding. Remember, so often these things are invisible to the physical sight because they cannot be shown on the physical plane. Vibratory rates, faculties, and functions cannot permit it until you arrive at a certain stage of consciousness. When you arrive at that great understanding you will know how you enter Retreats, how you enter many places where you would like to go. Again, I say, take the consciousness: I AM THE PRESENCE HERE AND NOW!

*   *   *

Accept what you decree for yourself and what you desire for yourself. Take that consciousness as you say "I AM the Perfection of life," and on that instant within your heart center accept yourself as perfect, and see yourself a perfect being. If you say: "I AM determined to be happy and harmonious," then see yourself, right in your heart if necessary, laughing and smiling, and see yourself happy and harmonious.

It is the acceptance on the instant that you make the call that causes you to become the thing. It is the thing that little children do so naturally and beautifully without any questioning or instantaneous doubt thrown in, as the more mature mind will do. A little child will accept instantly. If you say to him: "You are a good boy," and he may have been a naughty boy, you will notice the little face light right up, or go into a little spoiled pout, but nevertheless he instantly receives the acceptance within himself as being a good boy, and in a sense it is wonderful, for the reprimand has come directly to the child and it is a good lesson for him not to be naughty again.

You can say to a child, "We are going to the show," provided the child is of the age that he knows what a show means, and you will see a glow come on the face. He neither thinks of money, transportation, nor clothing, nor whether anybody is going to be annoyed; but the human sense, you see, when you say, "Let us go to the show," lets several things fly into the mind: you are going with somebody else, what will you wear, and so on. That is a rather crude example but nevertheless it is that acceptance that must come before you can enter the Kingdom of Heaven. "Ye must become as little children" in accepting that you are the Presence before you can enter the King's Domain, the Great Dominion of Light.

Understanding is a very great law and one must know the Law of Understanding before he becomes Master. You come into Understanding right after the stage of Tolerance, and as soon as understanding establishes itself you experience the sensation of Joy. Now this Joy must be controlled, and it is that Joy that is witnessed by unenlightened ones and those who are going through struggles that almost causes them to turn against you; but if that Joy is released with Wisdom, with the Understanding that you have acquired, it will be a blessing and others can absorb it, because when you enter this stage of Joy after having arrived into Understanding, you release a substance from your form that is different than in an unawakened individual. You release a Light that is very powerfully charged with the substance of the incoming Age.

In the heart is the core of that sun which has its counterpart in the etheric body, which is the true etheric anchorage of your I AM. When you go to your physical heart and think upon the golden Light or a Sun of Light, you attract the substance of your true heartself to pour out through you and penetrate the physical form.

Now your bloodstream plays a large part in the messengership of this relaying of the substance of Love, the Love that is anchored in your heart. You have heard Us say that one day the bloodstream will be filled with golden liquid Light, and that is so, and at that time when humanity does arrive at that state and has transmuted the red into the gold, at that time your own flag will have its stripes changed and the flag will be gold, white and blue.

Visualization

Turn your attention to the Silent Watcher. As your system is His body, so your own heart is to your system as He is to this system in which we live. Think deeply about the Great Silent Watcher. As you think about Him, see Him through your heart, through your physical sun, through the very heart, the very core of your system. Deeper within and at a higher rate, looking in that great tunnel of White Fire, you will find the Great Silent Watcher. Your own heart is the

Silent Watcher of your body. If you understand that you can comprehend the Silent Watcher of your system, the body that is your system.

It would be very wise to tell more people about the power of the color violet, and you will find that many highly illumined people will almost instantly say that they detest violet. It is then your opportunity to call for the direction of your Presence that it may be worded perfectly so that they may have revealed to them the many wonderful qualities, the substance, the healing activities and the high vibratory rate that comes from violet. In that way they will think upon it and attract through themselves the power of the Violet Flame, the Fire of Forgiveness. All must do that; they must have it to raise their own forms.

Some have gone to the extreme, trying to impress this point upon others, but that is not necessary. You will find that you say the right words as you speak to the individuals, and no two of them will be alike. Their wishes or their mannerisms, their attitude, often their appearance, etc. will give you the perfect clue or perfect way to speak to them; and it is quite in order to work along the same lines with revelations, especially towards black, for that is the absence of color, the absence of Light, and you are teaching Light, you are exposing Light, you are talking Light. Again, working with your Presence you will say the right words to each one and in that way you are balanced at all times—balanced and understanding. You see you instantly know that and know that is the way it should be, and that is understanding, Cosmic Understanding.

Now again return to your heart center and be very clear in your own heart that you are the Presence. Repeat silently: "I AM the Presence." Hold that closely in your consciousness and the last thing as you relax before going to sleep, enter within your heart, expand that until it is a great Sun of Light—your entire system, your entire aura in that sun—and enter through the tunnel of Light toward the Teton, through your heart. Also, think of the Great Silent Watcher in your heart, deeper, ever higher, toward this great scintillating center of the Sun as if you walked through a tunnel into the heart of the Great Silent Watcher, and through that inner tunnel will pour to you out through your heart center, through the top of your head and your heart, this substance that is this expanding action of Light. It will penetrate every cell of your body from the top of your head to the tips of your toes.

*   *   *

Never hold back the understanding which you receive and never try to obtain these laws for yourself alone. In other words, as your cup is filled, give it forth. If you hold back it causes you to reembody. If you hold back what has been given forth by the Great Ones, and especially the Master Jesus, you become a thief. You must give of your Light. You must give of this Law and this substance which is given to you. You must give of it to others unconditionally. There are no reservations to be made under any circumstances, for what the Great Presence gives to you to give forth should be given out. If the Presence finds that you hold back what It has given to you to give forth to humanity, then It causes you to turn once more to the action called death and reembodiment. When you give this Law, which is the "bread of life" you give of this substance to humanity, you overcome death and you no more have to reembody, and you can live on and on in the physical form as long as you wish to serve, up to a certain point whereby your momentum becomes so great and your service so great and your vibratory Light so high that you cannot exist here any longer. At that time you then enter the plane of the body you have formed. You only exist in the body of which that plane is made.

This transition period, which is transpiring for the illumined ones of the Earth at this period, is very trying. It is difficult to know of your Light body, and it is difficult to know of your flesh form, but if you realize that this is the transition and the more you feed your Light body with the food of the next plane in which you are entering, the more powerful it becomes, and you know by that action that you are consciously lifting yourself out of the physical realm. You will be visible to mankind, you will be working here for some time to come, but you will not be of the physical plane.

*   *   *

The assistance is pouring from the Golden City. Think not these things strange that enter your mind and enter your world from now on. They are very real and they are the things for you to do. As many of you have been learning very recently, the more you stay in that consciousness known as "Except ye become as little children ye cannot enter the kingdom of heaven," the more you can receive your direction from your Presence and from the Great White Brotherhood, from the Golden City, and the Etheric Cities. These cities are so very real to each one of you and to many of humanity. It is the information and pattern of that which is to be in the New Golden Age. Many things will come to you with great speed, and in the consciousness of that joyous, tolerant, expectant attitude will you be the wonderful channel to fulfill these various things for the human race.

The great Light Rays which pour forth to the Earth from the Golden City and from the Etheric Cities are filled with ideas and substance which is a glory to behold. In the expectant attitude is the receptive vehicle which can bring these things forth for humanity. Up to a certain period there are certain things you cannot have for human use, as you well know, but if you can be patient in this understanding and fulfill the things that your form can fulfill, then these things can come to humanity very rapidly.

Call that your entire body raise in vibratory action. The work has been done so much around the heart and the upper portion of the body that often the visualization ends there and you forget to visualize the rest of the body in White Fire, so that the lower part of the body does not raise as far as the upper. Remember as you draw in the great Fire Breath into your bodies that when you do this consciously you are raising your forms. It is very wise that you do this consciously a few times every day. Think about it. Say: *"I AM the Fire Breath of God"* or *"I AM the Fire Breath of Creation,"* and *"I AM the Great Fire Breath illumining my entire being to the arisen form."*

As you do that and be natural about it, you will light up and expand, raising the vibratory action of your own form. The more you do it the quicker you will be able to travel throughout the world, by consciously going within and turning your attention to where you wish to be. It will raise the vibratory action of this form here, and you will step forth to the place where you wish to be and fulfill the service you go there for. You will lower the vibratory rate to have the appearance of the people and customs where you wish to be, and when you return, you will return the same way. This is very close to you. It is nothing fantastic or impossible, it is a natural law of your being, and it is as simple as breathing. Let your mind think about it and think about this activity that every cell of your being becomes accustomed to the new idea and accepts this for you. Then as it can transpire for one, it will spread very rapidly to others.

These things you must accept. You must be able to shut out the doubts and fears so accurately and so clearly that nothing stops your progress, and also remember when you turn your attention to this Light within your heart and expand the Light in every cell of your body, that you are building about you once again your own Wall of Protection, your forcefield of White Fire, which you had once and receded from it quite far, but now as you build it back you cannot lose it. Before it was a gift to you, and now you earn it consciously, and within that forcefield you are a conscious creator.

Your Wall of Light has been split apart and torn from you down through the ages. Now you live in it and you must realize it is energy acting. It is very powerful, and as it closes about you, you commence to live in a house of Light. That is consciously drawn substance and that substance is acted upon by you. It is your material to mold into that which you wish to do on the human plane, and it is that material which grows into the beautiful Causal Body, which causes your accumulated good to move into this magnificent area and circle about it and that causes you to move upward into it. Then from this great wall that you have around you, the great White Fire, you have your Causal Body, and it acts and you look like a Flame in a more or less egg shaped action of White Fire, and that is held like a ball in realm upon realm of your accumulated good. It has color and it has sound. It has that because thought and feeling are color and sound. Your Causal Body is stationary about you and your Light penetrates out through this. Your rays act as a pulsating glow which go forth in constant action through this great body.

There is to be no joking in a kidding way about this Mighty Law which you have learned and about the powers of this expanding action through you. I do not mean for you to be serious and fanatical about it, but I would rather say be serious about it than to joke about it. You are going to grow in the next few years at a speed that you cannot conceive of now. You are going to grow in consciousness, in understanding, in wisdom, at a tremendous speed. It is what you have been asking for. It is what you have been calling for, not only this group, but thousands and thousands of students of Light throughout the Earth. It will not be unusual. It isn't something which is just thrust upon you as a surprise and a gift. It couldn't come to you that way. If you don't want it you won't have it. If you do want it, you will have it. But it only comes through your desire, through your call, through your application. Anyone who says to you it is not necessary to make application, it is not necessary to work for these things, they will just come to you anyhow, do not listen to that kind of conversation.

There are those on the earth who seemingly receive information, assistance, and you might say, almost physical gifts without making hardly any effort—that is, it may seem that way to you, but remember, nothing comes to anyone if he has not earned it. It simply is not possible. It never did, it never will, it never can. It is not possible! Those who receive gifts, directions, visits from the Arisen Host, material things of any kind, guidance, illumination of any kind which seemingly look like gifts without being asked for, they have earned it in some previous life and they have released energy where they have served lifetimes in that service and it stands in their lifestream, it is in their Causal Body; it is energy that demands that the Flame within receive its due. And so that one has served, and served, and served and has arrived at a point in life's growth where things are almost handed to him or her on a silver platter, sometimes a very golden platter. Then those about him who see it sometimes feel offended and say that one received, and he doesn't, and that one does not seem to be doing so much. But you as students knowing this law, know better, and never again, when you see some one receiving, feel that he is being treated a little better than you. Just remember, it is service, and your service is the giving of this pure essence which you are to others, to other conditions, to other things, on whatever plane you are working. It is the giving of this essence which forms your Light Body. You must give to receive, and you must give, and you must give, and you must give!

Light consists of all things, all the qualities which you know are good. Light consists of Peace, Justice, and Harmony. It consists of Truth, Happiness, and Joy, and everything that you give of these qualities. You must give happiness, you must give joy. You must give peace, and harmony. You must give encouragement and patience. You must give tolerance, and you must give, and give, and out of that you grow. Out of that you shall see and step into the realm of the Arisen Masters.

XXII

BE A SUN OF LIGHT!

by Saint Germain

Beloved ones, rest assured that any Master will feel welcome in any household where harmony, beauty, order, and peace prevail, and where efforts are being made by the inhabitants of that household to create those conditions and make them a reality.

When you have some little thing drive in, when some little thing finds an opening in your armor, please don't give it any power. There was a time when each one of you found it most difficult to throw off periods of depression, failure, etc., but now how much more rapidly you are springing to your feet and calling to your Presence and suddenly finding peace and ease in your feelings and being able to perform your tasks as you should. Do you not see this is true mastery, that you are gaining dominion over yourself and all the earth, for you are at-one, and as you master yourself you have mastered the Universe, because it is all One. When you can completely master one little atom, you have in that instant mastered infinity itself, for does not the same law apply throughout? So learn these things. This is your schoolroom. This is the place where you learn.

Will you expand your mental horizon and open your hearts and see with Me, with the bigness of the Arisen Host, at the moment. Will you look across the vast fields, plains, mountains and seas which are this world and will you see with Me the teaming humanity which inhabits this planet. Now will you see with Me that these individuals who are here are fulfilling their life streams and that these individuals are eternal—they cannot be destroyed. Will you see that. They are here. They have been here many, many times before, some from other planets, some to complete their lifestreams upon other planets. This is an opportunity for them to serve here at this time. Do you see that? Then do you quite understand with Me that even though a war is a dreadful and destructive and appalling thing, there is no permanent destruction, there is only an altering of the form, for the individual is eternal. From that Light he came and into that Light he will return, and of the Light he is, and ever is he of that Light. I AM that Light sustained eternally.

Now if you can view with Me the world and the world situation as I have been speaking to you, you will attain a peace in your feelings, a calmness and assurance that regardless of the outcome of the day or the morrow, the Victory of the Light is absolutely certain. These forces of darkness, these evil, sinister things which seek to dominate humanity, to enslave at the will and whim of certain individuals, will cease! Do you not see that? They have no real power, only a temporary human authority which they wrest from others as a result of intellect, happenstance, and evil cunning; but they have no power, for that Light which is every man, was here before the man embodied and will be here afterwards, and is the man himself in embodiment. How then can the darkness prevail?

Watch yourselves, and view the political situation in the light of these remarks I have made to you. Stand with the Light, and stand firmly where you are, but do not be dismayed. Your dismay, if it occurs, will be an open door for darkness to rush upon you. Stand in the Light firmly, and with confidence know—*I AM that I AM now and always sustained forever by the Power of Light itself.*

Remember, one of the attributes of mastery is fully to use the knowledge and the wisdom which you have, without curiosity about the things that you do not know. It is quite all right to seek new knowledge when that new knowledge has a purpose, for then all things will be revealed to you, but just to accumulate additional facts is of very little value and often beclouds the issue. Think about that.

Use what instruction you have been given. Use it to the utmost, and when you have mastered what you have, more will be given. Rejoice in the magnificent postion you stand in today, and go forward to newer and ever greater victories!

*   *   *

As you stand alone in your I AM Consciousness, let each one stand as a Sun of Light. See yourself as a Sun of Light, your pristine colors of accumulated good about you, and see your hands spreading forth in benediction, the Light Rays pouring forth from the heart, head, and hands and pouring into mankind everywhere. I AM that I AM—awakening each soul in embodiment and all who are preparing to return; awakening them to the reality that God is within the heart, that this Wisdom and Light is the guidance which guides each individual.

Taking that consciousness, see yourselves as beings of Light, turning these Light Rays and this Mighty Focus toward Europe. First, see yourselves as Masters, the Great Masterful Perfection of the Christ Fire pouring forth from you. See the Light Rays pouring forth as a great body towards the heart of Europe, first into France, and then like great searchlight rays, flood over Europe, through Italy, constantly repeating: I AM that I AM. Awaken to the God in your heart! Turn within and receive your pure directions! Focus those Light Rays toward Russia and in that outpouring consciously send forth Peace! Peace! Peace! Also, see the Violet Fire spring up where these rays touch each country. The great action of the purifying element through France and Germany, through the heart of Europe, and then see that spread across Denmark, Sweden, the Scandinavian countries, through the British Isles. Then see that expand into Asia and the Far East. See the Light Rays pouring forth, especially assisting all those holding the Light in every country. See them touch upon the points of Light there and intensify and help. Give all the Great Ones who are the focus in those countries assistance. Let them know we are aware of their work. See the Light penetrate through all of China, India, sweeping across the entire country, and in Japan. See the Violet Fire penetrate far below the Earth's surface and flush through the countries where disease is breaking out, and raise the consciousness of the people, that they may have Illumined Consciousness, a Consciousness of "I AM that I AM."

See the purification process penetrating through the oceans, the Atlantic and the Pacific, until the Light Rays reach all the waters. See everything penetrated with Violet Fire, and then see it penetrate through the United States, the three Americas, Canada, and throughout the entire Earth, that lifting, purifying element of the Violet Transmuting Fire. See an intensified focus of it in Washington, D.C. and through the leaders of the various nations; and may the Power from the Great Central Sun and the accumulated force of the Great White Brotherhood expand and intensify the Fire of Forgiveness throughout the Earth. May that continue for days and days, raising and purifying, and may the release of Peace and Cosmic Understanding take the place of that energy which has been so misqualified, that it becomes purified and raised. May the I AM Consciousness penetrate through and take dominion.

In this consciousness, and in this Focus which holds this Cosmic Fire and goes forth by our conscious attention upon it, send forth your thoughts and your feelings the very feeling and determination that war shall cease, that those countries which have seen such drastic warfare heretofore will not have to experience that again. Silently call to the Great White Brotherhood to guide you and show you what you can do in thought, feeling, and action that will help, that there need be no more war on Earth.

Visualize the Etheric Cities in the atmosphere above as becoming realities here to your physical senses on the physical plane, by thinking about them, accepting and visualizing your entering them, and that substance becoming active here.

See the planet without any animals. In that consciousness, if you can visualize the entire Earth stripped of the animal kingdom, you can visualize how it has raised the consciousness of man, how you would stand at a different level, and that low vibratory action transmuted. Accept these things in your thoughts and feelings, in your conversation, and in your visualizing, that these things can come about.

Read well the "Seven Planes of Consciousness" given to you. (See *Step By Step We Climb*) Therein it says that you will have to learn how to contact the Arisen Host, and such things as being above the temptation of misusing this power. Not one of you present need have any fear that you do not know how to contact an Arisen Master. Each one has consciously and on many occasions done so. Some by vision, some by feeling, some by hearing, and some of you by ecstatic moments, moments when you have fulfilled a service consciously requested and directed through you by one or more of the Arisen Host, and upon receiving the gratitude from the Master or Masters, you have been raised to that consciousness which makes you want to hug the whole world. In that moment you consciously faced the Master, on occasion the Masters, and if you were to record the various instances, the various moments when trancendent things have happened for you, if that were to be recorded on paper, or a record in words, or in some way that you could refer back to it, you would find that they have been quite numerous. But because so many outer things take your attention, and so many so-called disappointments seem to drive in, it has not the power to act, for the disappointments, which never should be but do happen, or the physical set-backs in some way are felt, and the reason they have so much power in your world is because of your functioning on the physical plane, so naturally they are the things closest to your consciousness. But in some way make a physical note of the wonderful things which happen for you. We call them wonderful because We are trying to make a definite point. They really are the natural things that happen for you, but to the human they are seemingly wonderful.

The action of the Lotus Flower that is in the room is transcendent. The reason it takes the shape of the lotus flower is because of your love and your desire to understand and be this Law. The center of this flower is a deep gold and acts like a mighty cushion in its soft velvety upflowing, for the substance of your understanding of this Law, which is

Wisdom, has accumulated as you have followed tonight, and you each act as a white petal. In one way it is more like a great daisy but the petal is shaped as the great lotus flower, and this up-pouring, the petals turning upward, is like a great saucer that is pulling up its wisdom, the saucer full of Wisdom and Light.

If you can intensify the good points within you, then give love and joy and happiness and gratitude for them, whether they be one a week or ten a week, or five a day, or whatever they may be, but in that acknowledgement and that gratitude that you find those good points, you will soon grasp how you reach through to the Arisen Master. The good points that the Masters pour, that is, the good points which you pick up which tune into the Master's aura, are opening a direct channel to a Master. When you feel that so-called charge go through you, or that sensation as of so-many needles penetrating through you, or the so-called pressure in various points of your body, such as your head, the back of the neck, and through the great focal points in your body, or when you feel those sudden bursts of joy, a sudden feeling of ecstasy or happiness, qualify it quickly with peace, self control, alertness, gratitude and humility. Almost always that is an opening of one or another of the Arisen Host working through you and it is the way your physical mechanism picks it up. Be very careful not to requalify it. Be alert. You are learning the use of Light Rays, and are using them.

You are learning to use forces, Cosmic Forces, and there are many forces. You are learning that you are being used by the Elder Brothers who guide humanity, for They in turn are used by Cosmic Beings who guide Systems, and They are used by those higher who guide galaxies, and so on. As you are used in this manner, you yourself learn to direct Light Rays and lines of force that are used by others of humanity who are coming upon the Pathway who one day will be in the awakened consciousness, and then one day Master. Accept your mastery and accept that you are in touch with the Masters.

Be patient with those that you work with in other fields.

Be patient with others seeking the Light. Knowing the law of patience and tolerance, let that go forth to each and every one you work with.

If you will silently accept your heart as a cup, the edges formed like the lotus petal, reaching upward, filled full to overflowing with Golden White Fire pouring and pulling upward through the heart center, you will help to assist your own form to absorb and utilize this upraising, up pulling action for you. As never before you will understand the Christ Consciousness after tonight. Call through your heart for this to be illumined to you and expanded through you until it is so clear that never again will you ever question what is the Christ substance. I tell you it is as clear as crystal in this room tonight.

Now see this Sun go forth and light up the entire Earth, and may this Christ Consciousness penetrate into the heart of Europe, Germany, France, through Czechoslovakia, and all the low countries, Greece, Turkey, up through Sweden, Norway, Denmark, down through Spain, through the British Isles, again through Russia, through all of Asia, Africa, India, the Far East. See the Light penetrate through the waters, through Australia, the Hawaiian Islands, the Philippines—see all penetrated with this new Light—the United States, the three Americas, Canada.

See all small, petty things dissolved in this new consciousness, all greed, lust, envy, and the new Light, the new understanding burst forth, the Oneness, the humility, and the consciousness of the Masters, that can only come through by the students' Light making it come through, and you are part of that group of people.

Hold the picture of the perfect world·in mind, all the Arisen Host—you and I, Masters all. Hold the picture of perfect harmony, the perfect system here. Visualize each one held in his own aura of White Fire, about you enfolded in a protective radiance of the blue-green energy and substance. Take the consciousness: *I AM humble. I AM obedient. I AM determined to be the Light. I AM determined to go forth Master on Earth!*

XXIII

NEW YEAR'S EVE WITH THE MASTERS

by Arcturus

Students of Light and Truth: Tonight a new precedent is being established for the children of Earth. Heretofore, for many long centuries of time, as you know it on this planet, We who function in the Unobstructed Universe and who are concerned with the activities here, have been accustomed to meet in certain places secretly that We may radiate and direct energies to the wayward children of Earth.

Tonight, My beloved children, We who function at a level above the human are coming forth at this one spot in the human octave and are establishing here at this focal point an activity which will be carried on from this time forth with ever increasing power. Instead of remaining in Our Retreats on this eve, We are going to pour Our energies and the energies from the Royal Teton through you remaining in the physical octave who are gathered here for this purpose.

Beloved ones, I trust you have come here with the proper motive. If you have come out of idle curiosity to see what was going to transpire, it would be better that you had not come. If that should be the case, prepare yourselves as never before between now and twelve o'clock that your motive may be purified. If you have come because you desire to serve the Light, because you desire to serve the Presence of Almighty God and We of the Arisen Host who are present, and these who are in the physical octave and represent Us; if your desire has been to love and to serve them, and Us, then indeed you are most welcome and the benefits and blessings you will receive will be beyond your fondest dreams.

We have caused an hour to be set aside this eve which does not belong to any time and We have taken it for Ourselves. Humanity has been playing with every force, with every substance, with every thought that they can lay their hands or their minds to. Humanity has been experimenting with forces of life and forces of Light which are tremendous beyond their childish imaginings. Today they have tampered with certain forces in the universe which, if released, will turn upon humanity and remove it and this school room from existence. These so-called scientists who have failed to recognize the great creative Principle of Life, Light, and who continue to persist in experimenting with atomic energy, may remove themselves and this planet from existence. But inasmuch as humanity has seen fit to tamper with these forces, including daylight saving time, We are taking the hour and using it for a release of Light upon this planet and in this location which will accomplish what will appear to be miracles. Here is an hour then that in human consciousness does not belong to the old month or to the new, in fact, nobody can find just where it is. We have your Great Friend Saint Germain to thank for this hour.

Now, beloved children, you must stop accepting appearances! You must cease giving power to things which are less than perfection! As you value your progress will you please remember and recognize and practice these things. You can command in the Name of Almighty God and the Universe itself will serve your slightest wish! Do you think that We are to be put off by puny human concepts? I tell you, beloved friends of Light, *command with authority!* You and you alone must command perfection into your world! Why longer continue to accept imperfection? Why longer misqualify this Great, Pure, Limitless Energy which pours in and through your body?

I realize the difficulty that always appears to stand in the way to your peace, your confidence, and your progress, but I too, blessed ones, long centuries ago, faced the same difficulty that you face today in your human experience, and I say to you, blessed children of Earth, *acquire a new set of values.* Recognize those things that are *real* and those things that are unreal, and when you place your faith and your confidence and attention upon those things that are real you will go forth with certainty and the difficulty that has seemed so over-powering will disappear.

I am going to say one more thing about this evening. Humanity has for a long time considered that New Year's Eve was a time for revelry, celebration and a letting down of the normal restraints and prohibitions which otherwise pre-vailed. This evening, the last of the old year and the first of the new year, is an evening of most deep, sacred significance with respect to your entire planet. It is an evening to be approached with great reverence and with great under-standing. The day will come when humanity will recognize this evening for what it is and will assist Us in bringing about the greatest possible release of love and joy and Light at this time of the year.

Let Me make this emphatically clear: Our activity is not a long-faced activity. We are not a group of sour featured men and women just because We have made Our ascension. On the contrary, We have learned the fullness of the meaning of Love, and what else do you suppose makes one happy? If you could see for just one twinkling of an eye the unhappiness, the loneliness, the fear, the greed, the lust that comes about as a result of misqualification of the activity of love you would join with Me as never before in assisting humanity to rise up out of its limitations, and particularly at this time of year.

XXIV

THE ANSWER IS LOVE
by Lord Maitreya

Dear ones, I know that you know this is a great honor being bestowed upon you, and indeed it is a great honor being bestowed upon Me, for I have striven through many centuries to find a group of people, and especially one or two individuals who could be strong enough to assist in this work in this fashion. There were some who endeavored previously to be channels for Me and there were others who, through one activity or another were made to believe that they would be a rebirth of the Christ, as was at one time represented by My activity. Blessed ones, I want you to know unmistakably that even though I did assist your great Friend and the Benefactor of mankind, Jesus the Christ, still never did I do the work for Him. Always He made His own effort and achieved His ascension in the manner that has been told you, especially in the manner that has been described in one of the books that most of you have read, (*Prince of the House of David*).

Dear ones, the answer to your problem, whatever your problem may be, is a simple one. It is Love. That is the answer. All the other things, all the other teachings, the various problems as they may appear, can be solved by various manifestations of Love, but Love is the answer. O what a terrible thing, what a dreadful thing that the people of this planet do not understand Love. There, dear ones, was the fall of man, and as man learns to understand Love, he rises again into his victory. It is as simple as that. Love is the key, and you cannot attain your victory unless you learn to master Love. Love is a feeling, but it is also a thought. There is a pattern that proceeds Love, but Love is the energy and the power of life itself that can and must flow from your Presence through your physical body and out into the world as a blessing to humanity. This simple act of loving you must learn to do at all times.

You have so many, such infinite opportunities to do this simple thing, yet so often, due to the pressure of this very dense and heavy atmosphere, and due to the distractions of so many noises and colors, emotions, etc. your attention is taken from the simple activities of life and you become confused and sometimes disheartened when you do not see the perfection that your heart desires.

Call your Presence into action! At the slightest suggestion, how many times a day do you see something that is less than perfection and say something about it, express yourself in some way, perhaps even silently you say, "O, this person made a mistake," or "that person's house needs paint," "this one needs a new car," "I need a new dress," or whatever it is, and your consciousness takes on an activity of lack, a belief that imperfection is manifesting. You accept that a house which needs paint is less than perfection, and you accept that some one who performs an act that is not perfect, is not perfect. But dear ones, why not charge yourselves to call your Presence into action to release the thing that is required at that moment? When you see someone who requires a new car, instead of criticizing that one in your mind, or just idly passing it by, leap into action, call your Presence to bless that one and to release into his hands and use a perfect car. That is your privilege, nay, that is your duty, that is the obligation that you who are students have to life, to your own Presence, and if you work under My radiation that is the obligation you will have to Me. You must charge yourself to be ever alert and aware of what goes on, taking every prompting as a call to duty, every suggestion that reaches your mind as an opportunity to release Love in your call.

When you see some one who requires something, turn to your Presence and give from the Presence to that one, whether it be lack of health, lack of money, lack of friends, a lack of anything, whatever the appearance may seem, the important thing is to turn to your Presence. Call the Presence into action and let that Love from the Presence flow out as a

gift of Light and Love to that one. If you will do this, if you
will practice this, your lives will become so beautiful that you
will live in a garden of beautiful thoughts and feelings and
you will manifest mastery right here and now! The desire to
know Truth is not knowing it. Seeking for the Truth is not
the Truth itself. You must call the Presence into action for
others as well as for yourself.

You must learn to live beyond the little cramped worlds
that you find yourselves in. Stop thinking of yourself when
you say "I AM." Think what it means—what it means to you.
Recognize that the I AM Consciousness, which is the true
Universal Consciousness of God, is a consciousness where
you accept no separation between you and God and between
you and every other human being. When you say "I AM" you
have taken on the responsibility of all your brothers and
sisters in the Light; therefore, you must learn and practice
these things. It is not enough to know them, you must apply,
and that is one of the activities of Love, the giving of your
calls in service to others.

The activity of Love, however, has many, many facets. It
is the cohesive power of the Universe that holds the Universe
together. It is the breath that causes the Universe to have life,
and it is the Breath of God itself. The love that you have for
your Presence must be a very real and tangible thing. You
cannot achieve victory, you cannot achieve your ascension
until you have learned to have your love flow out to your
Presence in a very tangible and very real way. It is not enough
just to think of your Presence. Think of this Great Father
who has created you. Think of that Light from whence you
came, and then give yourself in your entirety back to that
Light. Let your gratitude, your adoration fill your heart, and
when you do, you will begin to know the meaning of the
ascension and the meaning of Victory.

Since you still occupy physical bodies and these physical
bodies of yours have various appetites and desires, various
centers of energy which are important, it is imperative that
you learn to master those centers and master those bodies so
that you can become the fullness of life in your own personal

victory. This is never an easy matter for the individual at this level of consciousness. You are, at this level, creatures of sensory activity and, of course, being at this level, you must learn to master these senses, to control your attention, to control these centers of energy within your body, for when you have done that you can begin to learn what mastery is like.

For a long time nothing has been said to you concerning the activity of sex but I am going to mention it to you because it is a very important activity that you must understand and know about thoroughly. This activity of sex, these tremendous drives that you have as men and women here is for a purpose that is wholly good. Of course these activities are extremely powerful and because of their power at the present time they have seized upon the attention of humanity to a very large degree. This you will have to overcome in your own lives and in your own experiences, and also with humanity as you work with others who truly seek the Light.

Dear ones, please know for all time that you cannot indulge yourselves with a sensory waste of this God-given energy and at the same time go forward into mastery. Please understand, We know the tremendous power of these basic urges that you have and We do not criticize or condemn when an individual is unable or seemingly unable to master himself or herself at any given moment. Nevertheless, We know the law, and these energies which you have in your beautiful bodies can be raised and transmuted into the Living Essence of Life itself, which can and will take you into your ascension. You cannot attain permanent victory until you have learned to transmute that energy. Notice, I did not say "repress" that energy, "transmute" is the word.

You must learn to love truly, and the release of love from your precious selves to one another, when it is truly love, does not require the sex activity. Then what is sex for? Of course sex is for the purpose of procreation, or bringing into this world other human beings for reembodiment. That is what it is for. Right now the important thing for you to know and to remember is this: The use of the sex function for sense gratification is waste of energy which will simply delay your progress. It is not wrong, dear ones, it is merely a waste of energy. You must not look at it as a sin or as something evil, but you must look at it instead as a golden well from whence you can lift the Living Waters of Life itself and raise that energy into your heart and into your brain. When you have experienced the ecstasy of Divine Love you will know that the sex function is simply for what I have told you and for nothing else. Let Me assure you, as you raise your energies and learn to pour forth love from your heart, which is the proper organ for the release of this energy of which we speak, the release you will have, the thrill you will experience and the satisfaction that will be yours is far greater in just one instant than all the sense gratification in the world.

We know that there is a great service to be rendered by the young people who will be drawn into this activity here and hereafter in the bringing forth of new and blessed ones into embodiment, and please, as you value your progress, do not criticize the activity of a student of Light who has not as yet learned full mastery of one activity! Surely if you examine yourself closely you will find that somewhere you have not quite learned full mastery.

I have mentioned this concerning sex because it is extremely imperative at this time that you who are My students learn and thoroughly understand just what this means. I wish you to be masters of Love, I wish you really to understand the activity of Love, and you cannot fully understand it if the feeling of sex consciousness constantly rises before you. If you have feelings or misunderstandings concerning it then you cannot be master of Love. Your feelings must go and Divine Knowledge must be used. Practice, practice Love. Let the energy, the release from your heart go forth to everyone else. Do not be afraid of Love, it is the activity of God Himself. Surely you know that that which comes from God must be good. Do not fear these things. Practice Love! Practice Divine Love!

As the vibratory action of your bodies is raised you will notice changes taking place in your world. Some of them you will understand, some of them you won't, but the changes will be there. O dear ones, do not be led astray in seeking to observe the changes. Just be at peace and know that they are taking place. You do not have to look within your physical body and observe the blood flowing through your veins to be convinced that it is happening, do you? Yet it is going on every day, every minute. It only takes an amazingly short time for all the blood in your body to circulate completely through your body, but you are not aware of it, yet that change continues and it is never the same as it was before. Now as the rates of vibratory action increase for you, other changes will take place which, if you could observe you would see that your life is a series of concentric circles in which your love expands and brings you into greater understanding, greater peace, greater happiness.

Do not seek manifestation, dear ones, it is the open doorway to disaster for you. O how many times, I think perhaps more than any other one thing, the desire for manifestation has been the downfall of various students. Of course they are not lost, they merely drift around for a while for more manifestation until they learn that is the way of sorrow. Do not seek it! Seek the Kingdom of God, the Light within you, and all else will be added.

Most of these things that take place you do not see. Can one of you here tell Me the rate of vibratory action of your physical body? Would one of you know if it were increased? Of course not! Then why be concerned? Just be natural, normal, healthy, happy people. Do not seek the thrill of feeling Light course through your body. It will happen and you will feel it, but don't seek it. Do not seek the manifestation. Let your love and adoration go to the Light itself. Turn your attention to your Presence and recognize what It is. That is your eternal obligation to life.

XXV

THE SIMPLE PATHWAY TO HEAVEN

by Lord Maitreya

Blessed ones, may I tell you a great secret? So many times in your application you look for the result, and when you do not see that result forthcoming instantly you feel that in some way you have failed, but that is not the case. Your progress is determined by the energy that you release. It is determined by the effort that you put forth. The release of the energy, the effort, the love that you pour out is the actual accomplishment. The thing that you seek to accomplish, though it may seem important to you, and may be from many standards, is still of passing value, but the energy that you release is your victory. That which pours forth from you, when you permit it to pour forth unobstructed, will raise you into your everlasting victory.

O blessed ones, be at peace in your feelings, and if you find that for a moment you are not at peace, go to your Presence and let that Light from your Presence flow forth to remove from your world any feeling of inharmony or discord. I know that in stating it, it seems like such a simple thing, as all the laws of life are in reality simple, yet as you learn to obey these mighty simple Truths your world can be purified, harmonized, and raised until you truly become at-one with yourself. This is not an abstract statement but a statement of simple truth. To be at-one with yourself is to manifest perfect health in every fiber of your being; to find your heart, your mind, your body attuned and ringing the same cosmic note of Joy and Happiness. This can be done so easily, and because of your great determination to see it through it is very near for all of you.

Those of you who find that from time to time you are called upon to spend long hours by yourself, call to the Presence during those hours and learn to live at-one with

Almighty God. It is during those hours when people have a tendency to feel alone that temptation comes and humanity individually in its search for companionship is often tempted to go astray. An idle mind, you have heard, is the devil's work shop, and indeed it is true. When you discover that you have time on your hands, rejoice, for time, though it has no permanence insofar as We are concerned, from your stand-point is a very precious thing. Only a certain amount of it do you have. Every hour, every minute, every second is precious, for once gone it does not return to you in this embodiment nor ever again. Time passes for you in the physical octave and you must indeed make full use of every moment. You can make no better use of your hours and your minutes and your seconds than in loving God and in loving your fellow man.

Please resist the temptation of gossip. It is so easy to say something about another when that other is absent; it is so easy, but it is the way of the human and not the way of the Master. When you have something to say to some one, whether it be good or bad, say it to that one in love, in happinesss, and in joy, and do not seek another to hear your tale, but abide in that great stillness in you in which the power of love is generated and the opportunity of service is experienced.

My love flows out to you in an unending stream and I do not judge you, I do not judge your actions or your thoughts or your feelings; I only love you. Dear ones, if you will begin practicing this which I do, you will begin experiencing My Joy too. O it isn't easy. The human rises up and tells you this and that and the other, but learn to put it aside! The human must be put aside! We are moving into an age in which evolvement at the spiritual level is essential. You must, therefore, practice the utmost moral integrity, and it begins with learning to control your speech. You cannot be master if you find yourself saying unkind words to others. That is as much an immoral act as stealing, or telling an untruth. To be moral in a spiritual sense you must learn to use words of love only for blessing. I know, dear ones, that it is easy to follow the promptings of the human and it is seemingly difficult to follow the promptings of the divine.

You have within you both of these forces acting: the Presence, which knows no opposition and can supply without limit all the energy you require to become perfect, and you have within yourself the human, a creature of appetite and sensation demanding attention, clamoring to be satisfied. Your attention is your own. You can put it where you please, and *where your attention is there will your desires be.* As your desire flames up, if your attention is upon your human, then your human will be that which receives the power and energy of God; but if your Presence is the center of your attention, the energy of the Presence returns quickly to the Presence, then you have fulfilled the Law of Life. In this fashion you can purify your thoughts and feelings, and especially may I suggest that you learn to purify the spoken word. Remember that the word you speak is the grail in which your thought and feeling have been placed. An unkind word contains both thought and feeling, and it will live. Only create the beauty and perfection that you truly desire in your own world.

You cannot build perfect buildings with imperfect material. But recognize this: You are not building a physical edifice here in this which you are doing, you are building an inner temple that is invisible to human sight, and you are building it out of the substance of your own love and energy. If your love and energy is clouded and confused because of human thoughts and feelings of less than perfection, then your temple, which is also at the inner levels, will not express the beauty and the perfection that you so earnestly desire. You must be perfect within yourself and then you automatically manifest that perfection in physical expression. The task which you have for yourself is to make yourself perfect within. The law of like producing like will bring about the perfection you desire in the physical world.

Never admit that you are too tired to make your calls. Never admit that there isn't enough time or that you have a lack of energy. O dear ones, you have no lack of energy for what you really desire. If some one suddenly came to you and handed you your eternal victory, do you think you could really feel happiness and joy? I think you could. If some one suddenly came and handed you enough money to give you a new house, or a whole wardrobe of clothing, do you suppose in that moment you could express happiness? Of course you could! But that is only a reaction to stimulus. It is only an effect produced by a cause. But you are a being of cause and you must so control your world that you become only a being of cause. When you do that, and it is not difficult, you will go forward like a Light blazing with Purity and Beauty and bringing Harmony and Happiness to all whom you touch. All these things are real, and so important. So many are called, so few respond, but as you gain your momentum in this tremendous thing that you are doing you will sweep all obstacles before you and rise into a Happiness and Freedom of which you little dream. O it can be done! It has been done! It *must* be done by each one of you!

The path is long and the way seems narrow, but the joy of traveling it is the only permanent joy that you can experience in this physical octave. Did you know that? Other joys are transitory, but the joy you have in the release of energy that sends you forward into Light is permanent. Think about that. Do not grasp at the physical thing, grasp the Light. Seek always Light, and then the fullness of Love and Victory will be yours.

From this day forward I want each one of you to know and to feel, and say to yourself, if you have any doubt: "Maitreya loves me," and you will experience, when you speak My name, that proof of Me. This is more than just a spoken word, which, if you could see it, is filling this room, filling you, your heart, your consciousness. Call that it may be sustained for you, that you may go forward free from anything else than the perfection which your heart desires.

Dear ones, your steadfastness is the imperative thing today. So many truly blessed ones begin an activity and then when the way seems difficult or long they weaken and begin to wonder if they are on the right path, and then presently they grow discouraged and disheartened and their efforts cease. Today it is imperative that you learn to keep on and finish that which you begin. Sometimes the way seems difficult and sometimes you do not receive the encouragement that you think should be yours, but truly, beloved ones, you are walking the pathway that will take you forward to mastery, and encouragement is not always possible else mastery could not be won. You must learn to rely fully on your own God self, recognizing that All Powerful, All Pervading Presence in everything that you do, everywhere that you go, accepting that Presence as the only power that can act, not only in your world but in the world of everyone that you come in contact with, and it is wise to remind yourself of this activity at all times.

Give no appearance power in your world. Instead, rejoice! Rejoice that the Light of God fills your world and all things are made perfect in you. Accept it as an accomplished fact and so live that it is indeed a reality. This is the simple pathway to Heaven. It is the simple pathway to Perfection, and before this Blazing Light mankind will come to bow. Do you think We do not know what We are doing? Sometimes I know that you do not feel Me or the Presence of another Master and you doubt and wonder sometimes about so many things, but We know what We are doing.

If for a moment you see one who is doing something, or appearing to do something that you do not feel is right, please, will you refrain from criticizing. Will you not just *be* the Presence and accept your responsibility as an Arisen Master, even though you have not yet attained your victory. Will you not just make the call and be at peace and pour forth love and blessings to the one who seems to be transgressing at the moment? In the long ages that you have lived and in the long years ahead of you, these human things that seem so important to you at the moment, that cause you to be upset, are so insignificant. Rejoice that the law is yours and the pathway is open that you may go forward into your sure and certain victory.

You must learn, and I know to many it appears a bitter experience, that you arrive in this world alone and you will leave it alone. Companionship as you have here is a very precious thing and it is something that you must cherish, but the secrets that are revealed to you from the most High are yours and yours alone and they must be retained as inner experiences more precious by far than jewels or gold. Many times We have seen really blessed ones striving earnestly to make progress, making intense application, and then something is revealed to them and they cannot keep it to themselves. When that occurs their progress is not interrupted but other wonderful experiences they could have are not forthcoming at that time.

You have free will in everything that you do. You are here tonight of your own free will and your free will is important because without it you cannot develop into the God Beings that you desire to be. Cherish it but also understand it. Remember that you must be the master of your free will. Your free will cannot master you. If you let your free will control your every thought and feeling, then it becomes greater than you are and that is not true. You are the master and your free will is a tool that will assist you in making your decisions, but only if you master it and control it.

So many times you apparently lose ground because you do not completely see the reason for an activity. When the reason is not clear to you, call to your Presence. Do not seek to argue a point because that merely helps to establish that you yourself are not quite clear. Turn to the Presence and then call for illumination and wisdom, and then you do not have to argue because the point is made clear to you and everything will fall into a perfect pattern and the picture will be complete.

O precious ones, so many things you have learned. You have come a long way. Call that you be made pure in every way. Ask that your human desires or human intellect or human feelings be set aside and that those things be replaced with the feelings and the Light from the Masters' octaves, which can never be requalified with anything less than perfection. Do these things. It is more important that you *practice* these laws than it is that you know them. You must know them but you must also practice them, and even if you practice only knowing part of a law, that is important also. None of you dear ones has sufficient intellect to understand all of the law. It has been revealed to you in a greater or lesser degree according to your lifestream, according to your experience and desire. Do you all think you have learned the same thing? You have all been taught the same thing but each one has learned according to his or her own experience. You have learned much, but it is measured out according to what you desire and what you experience. Therefore, make intense application so your experience will be broadened and lengthened and you may truly be enlightened, illumined children of Christ Light, because it is only those who have practiced these laws who can accomplish their Victory.

Wisdom does not come to you at a single point. You do not gain your ascension by calling to the Presence to raise you into your mastery. You have not earned it and you will not have what you have not earned. You cannot be cheated, because this is an actual Law. *What you release comes back to you.* If you desire greater illumination, call for it. If you desire greater freedom, call for it and it will be given to you. *Nothing will be given to you without the asking, and nothing will be given to you until you are ready to receive it,* and then, at that moment, the heavens themselves will be opened and everything will be placed into your hands in an instant.

O dear ones, the need is very great, very great indeed, and the time is very short. You must put your human thoughts and human desires aside and be at-one with what is planned. Be at-one with yourself. Do not criticize yourself. If you feel that you have disappointed Me in a small degree, remember that one falling short of perfection is no worse than another and if you have done things you should not have done, call to your Presence, and forget those things and rise up and go forward into the Pure Light of the new day. Have you ever noticed, precious ones, that no matter what you do on one day, the sun's rays coming from the sun on the following day are just as bright and pure as the one you have ruined? That is the way it is with the Presence. Do you think the Presence holds a grudge because of what you have done? No, blessed ones. The sun is not concerned, but only shines forth, and the Presence is not concerned, but shines forth as a great Light. It is only man who is concerned. Do not criticize each other or yourselves, and when you face your Presence it is the dawn of a new day and the Light from your Presence is just as pure and plentiful as it was the day before. It is made new each moment that you love God. Think of it as it is.

A FIAT

CHILDREN OF EARTH:

    BE ALERT!

CARE NOT FOR PHENOMENA
LOOK NOT FOR MANIFESTATIONS
WORRY NOT OVER VAST WEALTH.
SUBDUE THE ACTS OF VANITY.
BRING PEACE THROUGH YOUR BODY,
BRING JOY AND SELF CONTROL.
BRING BALANCE, LIGHT AND HARMONY
TO A VERY TROUBLED WORLD.

    BE THE LIGHT!

BE THE BEACON THAT STANDS
WITH YOUR FLAME OF FIRE RAISED HIGH
AND YOUR KNOWLEDGE OF THE LAW OF LIFE
CLASPED CLOSE TO YOUR HEART!

    MOVE:

MOVE CONSTANTLY AMONG HUMANITY
GUIDING, LIFTING, SMILING, ENCOURAGING,
RELEASING THE GREAT WATER OF LIFE.
BE A LIVING EXAMPLE OF THE LAW!

– Lord Maitreya –

INDEX

Acceptance, Refuse acceptance of human conditions, 17, 140; Accept the Presence acting in everything, 110.

Action, Keep active, keep busy, 20; Certain amount of energy needs be released in the physical octave to keep balanced, 44; Keep yourselves occupied constructively, 51.

Adoration, Let your gratitude, your adoration fill your heart, 179.

Advice, It is such a temptation to try and step in and give advice. Do not do it, 45; Never suggest unless asked, 120.

Affirmations: Never tire of making your, 23; See Decrees.

America, To this land of Light, America, shall those seeking Light return, 81-4.

Appearances: Will lead you astray every time, 118; Stop accepting appearances!, 175.

Application, The solution will not come forth unless you make your application, 51-2; Go forward according to your application, 104; Do not listen to those who say it is not necessary to make application, 165; Your progress is determined by the energy you release, 183; It is more important that you practice these laws than it is that you know them, 189.

Arcturus: Chapters by, 149, 174.

Arisen Masters: Are above mistakes, 20-1; We cannot help you unless you accept our help, 30; Love of, 41; Sense of humor, 42; Never use a destructive force, 58; The radiation of the Arisen Master means so much to the student, 136.

Asking, Nothing will be given to you without the asking, 189.

Attention: Guard your, 66, 118; You become that upon which your attention is focused, 85; Proper use of the attention with your application, 105; Where your attention is there you are, 109; "The Law of the Attention," Chapter XVII, 136; Take your attention off human beings, 150; Where your attention is there will your desires be, 185.

Awakening, Many who will awaken as if from a drugged sleep and almost frantically turn to this Light, 16-7.

Blessing, When you see someone in need, turn to the Presence and give from the Presence, 178.

Body, 158; Call that your entire body raise in vibratory action, 163.

Brain, 156.

Business: Do not hesitate to call to Me in your, 135.

Cataclysms, 16, 92-3; Description of previous cataclysm, 122-4; Storms, earthquakes, fires and floods are man's self-generated discord, 138.

Causal Body, Nature of, 155-6.

Channeling, Approximately 85% of the people who inform you they have the All-Seeing Eye of God have, in reality, a very vivid imagination, 18; Call to your own I AM presence. Look not to channels, 32.

Christ, "You Are The Christ," Chapter XI, 85.

Civilizations: Rise and fall of, 104.

Cleanliness: Is next to Godliness, 70.

Concern: Opens you to many things, 19; Your only concern is to call the I AM Presence into action, and know all is well, 27.

Consciousness, The mighty power lying dormant in your consciousness, 73.

Confidence, Have confidence in yourself, 33; Importance of, 130.

Cosmic Light, Great release of Cosmic Light causing tremendous increase in vibratory action, 122.

Courage, Many, with enough courage and strength, can move serenely through a trembling world, 124.

Criticism, Refrain from criticizing, 187; Do not criticize each other or yourselves, 190.

Cyclopea: Chapters by, 100, 146.

Death: There is no, 86, 147.

Deception, There is no hiding of thoughts, motives, subtle human desires, 103.

Decrees, 71; One decree issued with feeling is of much more value than hundreds of empty decrees, 28; Do not feel in calling to the I AM Presence that physical effort is needed, 138; Acceptance the instant you make the call causes you to become, 159; Command with authority! 175.

Desire, Dangers of a tremendous desire for manifestation, 29.

Discipline, Approach the task of disciplining yourself in all seriousness, 88; The full power will never be released until you have learned to discipline yourself, 99; It is not up to you to discipline another, 120.

Discord, Not necessary to love discord or inharmony, 23; Never release a feeling against the person who is discordant, 61; Nip discordant thoughts in the bud, 95-6, 116; Those who have created discord and imperfection will find their creation returned to them, 122; Discord shall cease! 151.

Dispensation, The New Dispensation, 18; Possible for individuals to make the ascension even though their bodies were not raised, 146.

Doubt: And fear are your enemies, 37; Doubt and fear are always caused by a lack of faith in the Presence, 77; Doubt has to be removed before the full power of the Presence can flow forth, 97; See Fear.

Encouragement, Make a physical note of the wonderful things which happen for you, 171.

Energy: Qualification of, 44; You have no lack of energy for what you really desire, 185.

Evil: Avoid the appearance of, 124.

Example: Be the, 144.

Failure, There is no failure for any one of you at any time! 27, 72; See Victory.

Faith, Have Faith in the Light of God that Never Fails!, 124; Place your faith and your confidence and attention upon those things that are real, 175.

Fear, About 85% of the difficulty mankind faces is all in the imagination, 21; To fear the thing you must conquer is to give it power, 31; Doubt and fear are your enemies, 37; Fear is caused only by a lack of confidence in the Pure Christ within you, 47; Make your application to weed out doubt and fear, 115; See Doubt.

Feeling, The greatest percentage of energy of the individual is in the feeling body, 20; What you think and feel, even for an instant, creates, 24; Above all, I caution you to watch your feelings, 48; The All-Seeing Eye is one with your feeling world, 67; Your feelings are the important thing, 71; Govern your feeling world, 77; See Thought.

Fire of Forgiveness, Transmutes, lifts, and purifies, 156; See Violet Flame.

Foresight, Forewarned is forearmed, 69.

Forgiveness, When you go to bed, call off the names of those who have been disturbing you during the day and pour forth love and blessings to them, 94.

Free Will, Make no decisions for people. You must not interfere with the world of others, 45; You must be the master of your free will, 188.

Giving, You cannot give truly until you have given of yourself, 89; You must give to receive, 166.

God, Put loyalty to your own God Presence above the loyalty to any other thing, 36.

Godfre Ray King, "Godfre's Ascension," by Godfre, 127.

Gossip: Give no heed to any, 17; Resist the temptation of gossip, 184.

Gratitude, Never cease pouring forth love and gratitude to those who have assisted you, 87.

Great White Brotherhood: Motto of, To Know, To Dare, To Do, and To Be Silent, 65.

Guidance, Inner: See Inner.

Habits, Not possible for individuals to stop certain habits just by the use of sheer will power, 153; See Violet Flame.

Happiness, It does not take brains to win happiness, but love! 16; "Be Natural—Be Happy," Chapter V, 42; Happiness is the highest rate of vibratory action in the universe, 141.

Harmony: Is the Law of Love, 60; "Harmony—The Great Law Of Life," Chapter X, 75; Maintain harmony in your feeling world, 78.

Heart, Every individual must be ruled by the heart, 26; Your heart will tell you what the perfect thing for you shall be, 133; Your source is in your heart, 156.

Honesty, As you value your progress be honest with life, 75.

Human, Human consciousness reluctant to accept the truth, 134; Qualities of, 139.

Humanity, Must learn to live for one another, 151.

Humility, Let no one among you think that he or she has some part of God more than any other, 59; Do not believe you are better than anyone else because you happen to know the Law, 63.

Humor, Almost every Arisen Master has a sense of humor, 42.

I AM: The living fire of God, 123; I AM The Presence right here and now, 156; I AM is a consciousness where you accept no separation between you and God, 179.

Ideals, You are no greater than the thing for which you stand, 88.

Illumination: In the physical form takes place first in the brain, 157.

Indecision, One thing that is destructive is the constant indecision which faces mankind, 20.

Inharmony: See Discord.

Inner, "The Inner Realms," Chapter XIII, 100; If what you receive from the inner does not mean perfection, dismiss it as you would a serpent, 101.

Interference, Never interfere with a human being, 45.

Introspection, Study deeply yourself, and look at yourself honestly. You are your own greatest problem, 88-9.

Jesus: Chapters by, 34, 85; Statements by: I AM the Resurrection and the Life, 23; I AM the Open Door which no man can shut, 23; Ye must become as little children, 159.

Joy, Those who are able to maintain joy will find much less difficulty in obtaining their final Victory, 17; When you wish to know real joy, seek those who require joy, that you may give it unto them, 87.

K-17: Chapter VIII by, 65.

Kindness, Take time to be kind, 113.

Kubal Kumara: Chapter XV by, 121.

Lethargy: Do not accept the feeling of, 68; The laziness and lethargy of humanity is appalling, 108.

Light, Does not need to be defended, but constructive things in the physical octave do need to be defended, 27; A ray of light in the physical realm always moves as a result of thought, feeling, or of the spoken word, 28; Light is all the qualities you know are good, 166.

Loneliness, Those called upon to spend long hours by yourself, call to the Presence, 183-4.

Love, Divine Love is mighty and everlasting, 23; Love is Light, it is God, 47; When your heart is filled with Divine Love you will never go far astray, 85; Be not afraid to pour forth love, 89; If someone does something which you do not like, pour forth love and blessings, 94; "The Answer is Love," Chapter XXIV, 177; Practice Divine Love! 181.

Maitreya: Chapters by, 177, 183; "A Fiat," 191.

Manifestation, A tremendous desire for manifestation will move individuals into the dangers of the psychic realm, 29, 43-4, 182.

Mankind, "All Mankind Are One," Chapter XVII, 130.

Mastery: Cannot be achieved for you by others, 51; As you master yourself you have mastered the Universe, 167; When you have mastered what you have, more will be given, 168.

Meru, The God Meru, Chapter X by, 75.

Mistake, Keep your eyes off mistakes! 45; When you observe an individual who appears to be making a mistake, your obligation is to pour forth love, 55; Acknowledge a mistake to your Presence and do not tell anyone else, 75; Call to your Presence, forget it, rise up and go forward, 189.

Money, Nine hundred and ninety-nine people of of 1,000 are too lazy ever to have as much money as they need! 105-7.

Naturalness, Courage required to be natural, 19; To be completely natural is to be an Arisen Master, 42; Just be natural, normal, healthy, happy people, 120, 182; You may not appear in any way to be especially holy or untouchable, 152.

New Year's Eve: with the Masters, Chapter XXIII, 174.

News, Listen to at least one news broadcast a day, 114.

Obedience, "Illumined Obedience," Chapter II, 26.

Oneness, Turn your attention to the Oneness of all things, 58; "All Mankind Are One," Chapter XXVII, 130.

One-Pointed, When you are one-pointed you are without flaw in that which you are undertaking, 60.

Opinion, Do not have an opinion concerning one another, 26.

Opportunity, Those who refuse opportunities in the physical world will never make the ascension, 43.

Past, To the one who looks backward, disappointment will always overwhelm, 96.

Patience, Never be impatient with your progress, 76; Be patient with others seeking the Light, 173.

Peace, Goddess of Peace, Chapter VI by, 47; Peace will reign again upon this Earth, 49, 147.

Perfection, You cannot create perfection if you haven't it in your own world, 46; In your work do it absolutely perfectly or don't do it at all, 109.

Phenomena, Care not for, 29, 182, 191.

Physical, Importance of physical activity, 67.

Pity: The mistaken idea of, 141-2.

Power, When you begin to have power, use that power always with greater and greater kindness, 51.

Predestination: There is no, 69.

Prompting, A very quick way to find out if the prompting is from the human, 131.

Protection, Your own Presence, I AM, is the protecting power for you, 31; Your safety depends upon your own feeling world, 53, See Tube of Light.

Qualification, "Qualify With Perfection," Chapter III, 34.

Respect, No joking in a kidding way about this mighty Law, 165.

Responsibility, You will not fit yourself for the Arisen state by shirking your responsibilities in this world, 53.

Romantic, Cautions regarding romantic notions, 142.

Safety: See Protection.

Saint Germain, If you are sincere and will turn to me in love I can move mountains to protect you, 31; Chapters by, 15, 26, 47, 56, 67, 75, 92, 100, 112, 130, 136, 167.

Salamanders, Beings of the fire, 16.

Security, There is no security anywhere but in the arms of the Presence, 16.

Service, 100, Your obligation to life is to see perfection, to feel perfection, and to be perfection, 81; Service dear ones, is love, 90; Your obligation is to love and bless life, 119; Seek to learn what more you can do to assist others, 133.

Sexual practices: For the purpose of gratification is disobeying one of God's highest laws, 152; You cannot indulge yourselves with a sensory waste, 180.

Silence, 15; In the stillness is the great power, 58; Observe the Law of Silence, 66; Regarding inner experiences, 188.

Sincerity: Is one-pointedness, 60.

Sleep: Service rendered during, 94.

Speech: Control your, 184, The word you speak is the grail in which your thought and feeling have been placed, 185.

Steadfastness: Is the imperative thing today, 186.

Stillness: See Silence.

Sympathy: Dangers of, 50; See Pity.

Teacher, The work of the teacher is to get the student to accept in his feelings the Power of God, 117.

Thought, Before any real progress can be gained an individual must definitely govern his own thoughts and feelings, 21; See Feeling.

Transition, New Age: Chapter I, 15.

Tube of Light, You are building about you, once again, your own wall of Protection, 164.

Undines, Beings of the water, 16.

Urlando: Chapters by 42, 92.

Victory: Chapter IV by, 40; The Victory of the Light of America has been won! 56; Since you have begun the pathway to the Arisen Masters' octave you will succeed, you cannot fail, 72.

Vigilance, Do not ever let down your guard, 19.

Violet Flame, Remember that you as the human do not use it, 31; Mightiest cleansing, purifying power the Earth has ever known, 59; The high vibratory rate that comes from violet, 161; See Fire of Forgiveness.

Virtue: Is its own reward, 145.

NOTES

NOTES

NOTES

◆◆◆◆◆◆◆◆◆◆◆◆◆◆◆◆◆◆◆◆◆◆◆◆◆◆◆◆◆◆◆◆

Recommended Reading List

While there are many excellent books available from other publishers that would help the aspiring student, we especially recommend the following for those who wish to gain a greater understanding of the "I AM" Presence, the Ascended Masters, and the laws of Life. These books are *not* available from Pearl Publishing, but they can be purchased from your local bookstore or ordered directly from the publishers given below:

Unveiled Mysteries, by Godfré Ray King   Vol. 1
The Magic Presence, by Godfré Ray King   Vol. 2
The "I AM" Discourses, by Saint Germain   Vol. 3

Available from:
Saint Germain Press, Inc.
1120 Stonehedge Dr.
Schaumburg, Illinois 60194

---

*The Life and Teaching of the Masters of the Far
    East,* Vol. 1, 2, & 3,   by Baird T. Spalding
The Aquarian Gospel, by Levi
The Impersonal Life, —Anonymous
Christ in You, —Anonymous

Available from:
DeVorss & Co., Publishers
P.O. Box 550
Marina Del Ray, California   90294-0550

◆◆◆◆◆◆◆◆◆◆◆◆◆◆◆◆◆◆◆◆◆◆◆◆◆◆◆◆◆◆◆◆

♥♥♥♥♥♥♥♥♥♥♥♥♥♥♥♥♥♥♥♥♥♥♥♥♥♥♥♥

An Invitation

from friends of Pearl Publishing

We hope you have been inspired by this book. Pearl Publishing is an organization devoted to spreading the *Ascended Masters'* teachings. If you would like to know more about this great teaching, you may choose from the following books available from Pearl Publishing. Simply write us and we would be delighted to send them to you.

Step By Step We Climb (Volume 1). Twenty-four Ascended Master Discourses by Jesus, Saint Germain and other ascended masters. ISBN 0-9619770-1-9 (pbk.)

Step By Step We Climb To Freedom (Volume 2). Continuing instruction by the Ascended Masters in the great laws of life. ISBN 0-9619770-2-7 (pbk.)

Step By Step We Climb To Freedom and Victory (Volume 3). A collection of inspirational talks by Pearl which came as a result of deep attunement to the raised consciousness of the Christ principle. Pearl's insight and sincere application of these laws provide a simple explanation of the path to mastery. ISBN 0-9619770-3-5 (pbk.)

"I AM" the Open Door. Fourteen discourses by various Ascended Masters given to Peter Mt. Shasta. ISBN 0-9619770-5-1 (pbk.)

Pearl Publishing
of Mount Shasta

P.O. Box 1290
Mount Shasta, California 96067

♥♥♥♥♥♥♥♥♥♥♥♥♥♥♥♥♥♥♥♥♥♥♥♥♥♥♥♥♥